Life Stories of Bygone Days

Published in 2003 by the
Loddiswell History Group

Based on a collection of
interviews from recorded tapes
by Reg Sampson

Front cover photo:
Walter Kernick,
Dennis Sharland and Ned Lethbridge

Back cover photo:
Threshing at Lordswood, Churchstow, 1928

Life Stories of Bygone Days

Published by the
Loddiswell History Group, Lilwell,
Loddiswell Devon TQ7 4EF

Based on a collection of interviews
from recorded tapes by Reg Sampson

ISBN 0-9546005-0-9

Profits from the sale of this book will be given
to Local Heritage projects

Designed by Erica Anderson
Printed and bound by
EJ Rickards of Plymouth

British Library Cataloguing in Publication Data
a CIP record for this book is available from the
British Library

Distribution by Corporate Books
Telephone +44 (0) 1548 559 009
email sales@corporate-books.co.uk

Contents

Acknowledgments

The stories in the book are tributes to those who have participated in recording their life histories. Without their co-operation and enthusiasm I would have been unable to get a glimpse of so many lifestyles within a small rural village. Some had second thoughts and on more than one occasion I was greeted with " I bain't gwain to do it" but with some gentle persuasion I have been able to record many different life styles for posterity.

My thanks to the families who have turned out their personal photo albums and I would also like to express my thanks to the following people and organisations for permission to reproduce photographs and illustrations; The Cookworthy Museum, Kingsbridge, The Kingsbridge Gazette, The Western Morning News, J.C.Lawrence of Gosport for photograph of Royal Electrical and Mechanical Engineers in Blandford 1956, Andrew Lownie Literary Agent for a photograph from the book 'Submariner' by John Coote, and Copyright from J.Salmon Ltd., Sevenoaks, England for use of watercolour painting of Douglas Dakota Aircraft.

We have made every reasonable effort to track down the owners of every one of the photographs we have used in this book to ask permission for their use, but there are a few we have not been able to find.

Special thanks too for the generous grant received from the Local Heritage Initiative, under the Countryside Agency, which has enabled this book to be sold at a modest price.

The support and help from Erica Anderson in the design and production has been invaluable and thanks to my wife Betty for transcribing the tapes and compiling the tape headings and to John and Lucy Graham for their final proof reading.

Members of the Loddiswell History Group have given their valued support and encouragement, John Webber, Treasurer, Russell Baker, Karen Elliott, Hazel Lethbridge, Bill Penwill and Sue Sweeney.

Local Heritage *initiative*

Heritage Lottery Fund

Nationwide

The Countryside Agency

Preface

Nearly every aspect of our lives in the second half of the twentieth century has been recorded by newspaper coverage, television, films, photos and video but records of life experiences in the first half of the century are limited. Many of the stories that I have recorded relate to an era before electricity and mains water were installed in the home. Housework took up a considerable amount of the day and men worked six, and sometimes seven days a week doing hard manual work without any holidays. The old saying, "What you've never had, you never miss", certainly rings true.

Stories were passed down by word of mouth. Grandad reminiscing about the past was tolerated, but if only we had listened and remembered, our lives may have become richer and we would have benefited from their philosophy of life. In our present time the life experiences of our Grandparents will also be lost if they are not recorded before it is too late.

During, and for a while after, the two World Wars there was a void of news coverage and film was almost unobtainable by the ordinary citizen. I have been privileged in being able to record the personal experiences of several members of our parish who have contributed to the life of our village community. The wartime experiences of service men and women gives an insight into their traumatic wartime years, and were recounted as if they were only yesterday, and not sixty years ago.

People at home through that time endured bombing, hardships and sacrifices, but their indomitable spirits and determination helped to create the quality of life today. Some of the young men and women who were stationed here during and after the war married locally, and have made their homes here enriching our village community.

Basil Taylor

Basil's enjoyment of work and sport gave him an active and fulfilling life, but this did not distract him from his devotion and care of his family. As retirement drew near he suffered several severe illnesses and sadly died in June 2002.

Reg. **This morning I'm talking to Basil and Sheila Taylor. The house next door was one of the first schools in Loddiswell. Basil, you must have lived in Loddiswell all your life?**

Basil. Yes, I was born in Loddiswell, my parents lived in the little cottage between the Post Office and Mabel Goss's in Fore Street up the top end. I was born in April 1933 and we moved up to the Terrace next to Granfer Hine when I was three in 1936. Tom and Mabel Rundle ran the Turks Head, which is now the Loddiswell Inn and they, and their son, Owen, moved down to Town's Lane to Cross Farm.

Reg. **Where did your Dad live before he came to Loddiswell?**

Basil. They were living somewhere I'm not quite sure but I believe it was one of the Preston Cottages, because years later when I took him back he said he used to play football on the green there, there's a little green where the boys used to play. I know he spent all his young life there because he used to walk to Moreleigh three times on a Sunday for services and of course his Mother, Maria, and Father Amos went there as well. Dad left the Preston Coombe Farm and worked at Rake Quarry where he learnt to drive the stationary engines with old Bill Seldon who lived over at Well Street. He was in charge

Basil Taylor was born in Loddiswell and as a youngster sport took precedence over his school studies. As Joe Born his school master said, "If you put as much effort into your studies as you do into sport we would be better friends." Basil, however, went on to be a successful master builder and has left his mark in the workmanship evident in many houses in the district.

and my Father was learning his trade from him so that when he went to Brixham in the War, and later came back to Torr Quarry, he was the engine driver. He worked all the machinery at Torr Quarry, including the crusher; they used to truck the stones up on a rail track to the crusher, which Dennis Sharland was feeding.

Reg. **Your Mum, Dorothy, I remember when she was teaching at School. She was my first teacher and when she married your Dad we youngsters from the School sat at the back of the Church and watched the wedding take place.**

Basil. She left Loddiswell School when I was expected and then she didn't go back to teaching, although she taught the two Conran girls, privately, Daphne and Bridget. I used to go out there and play around while she taught the girls.

Reg. **When you were of school age you went to Loddiswell School?**

Basil. Yes, I was living at the Terrace at the time and I used to come down through the front garden, over the wall on an old ladder that old Jack Hyne, that's Ian Hyne's Father, had erected. I would go and pick up Ian and go to the School, which was held in the Church Hall, that was Miss Michell's Class. We did the first years there and then we went down to the lower school classroom with Miss Todd and then to Miss Common who was the head teacher. When we graduated to the top class in Loddiswell we used to have to get the milk from Little Reads, which was Cyril Harding's. We collected a big container and had to carry it up to the classroom in the Village Hall. We would dish out the milk up there or the teacher, Miss Michell would. Then we carried it down again, filled up at Little Reads and then we went down to the lower School and everyone was given a measure of milk in a cup, mug or whatever their Mother supplied for it. Everyone had their third of a pint of milk.

I went to Kingsbridge Grammar School from there, I spent four years in there from 1945 to 1948, it was really three years and a bit. We used to gather outside Butcher Walke's on the Bank in those days. Dennis and Les Walke were there and we all ambled down together, caught the train and then walked back from the train in the evening. It was a longish day, but we didn't know any different in those days. There were sports on Wednesday and Saturday afternoons, it was really a six day week.

Reg. **Were you involved in sports?**

Basil. Yes, very much so, I've got one cup here, won in 1945 for five sports in the Grammar School, I really enjoyed sports. As old Joe Born said, if I knew as much about school as I did about sport he would have been a much better friend to me. I left there on the twelfth of August 1948 and started to train as a mason, and I completed five years with J W S Scoble and Son. I think I am right in saying they had 157 employees, and when I started there were 34 apprentice boys. They had lorries and vans to take them around and I stayed there until I finished my trade apprenticeship. The Thursday after I left I was called up for my National Service.

Reg. **How much did you earn as an apprentice?**

Basil. The first week's wages I earned I gave to a man called Foster who was an ambulance driver in Kingsbridge, his son was an apprentice boy, and I bought a big old turnip watch from him. It was exactly one week's wages. £1.12.6

Left: "I went into the Royal Horse Artillery (RHA), actually it was tanks." 1954

(£1.60) I remember that.

Reg. **Then you went into the Forces?**

Basil. Yes, I went into the Royal Horse Artillery (RHA) actually it was tanks. I did my basic training and then I went to the Suez Canal and I was out there for the whole two years and came home in September 1955, I didn't see the real crisis that was at the end of 1955 and into 1956.

Reg. **I remember they sank a lot of ships to block the passageway in the Suez Canal.**

Basil. Yes, when we went out there first, we did armed guard up and down the Canal, or out in the desert, the Sahara, with our tanks trying to keep the peace on the ground. We were posted to accompany the boats going through, we had to go as armed guard from Zed to Suez and back. We had to stop anyone on the banks who were shooting at the crews on the boats going through. They started to block the Canal as I was leaving but I didn't see that. Our patrol was in a tank or armed vehicle, usually a 25-ton Cromwell tank, the guns were Sherman guns but I was an Out Post (OP) because of my meagre rank in the Army, for the want of a better description. We would go into the dessert for perhaps six or eight miles ahead of the guns and pick out targets and they would fire the shells over the top of our heads on to the targets. I was No 1 on the tank, Driver/Operator. My army training was as a wireless operator, but when I went out there I learnt tank driving because you earn more money a week doing that.

Reg. **The main Suez conflict was boiling up before the ships were sunk?**

Basil. Yes, definitely it was more of a Cold War than anything else. We were near Funnara, which was a big American air-force base with jets. It was quite funny really because Ian Hyne was out in the same camp as I was, but he completed his trade training and came home so he was exactly two years ahead of me. So as he came out of the camp to go home I went in the same camp, Walderley Camp. That was my army life.

I had learnt to ring the bells with Jack Eastley when I was twelve years old and right after the war when I left the forces the first thing I really remember when I came out was ringing for Parson Bliss, his last service and that was in October 1955.

I came back into J W C Scoble, they were forced to take me back for six months and then I had the option of leaving, getting the sack or whatever. It was at the time that J W C Scoble was closing down and they were getting rid of tradesmen left, right and centre. On a Friday night I stopped working for them and went with Jock Jordon to the job centre in Kingsbridge, that's what they call it now. That was on the Saturday and we got two jobs out at Galmpton building the sewerage works there for a firm called Squire of Newton Ferrers. We started there on a Monday and the other eight that left on the Saturday had no work, they were home on the dole that was in 1956.

Reg. But you didn't spend the rest of your time building sewerage works?

Basil. No, we graduated from there and I built several different places for them. Tom Brooking out at Chillington was looking for a mason full time, so I thought I'd cut the cost of travelling to Plymouth so I applied and got a job with him. I worked there for six years until 1963 and then John Webber and I set up in business together. We did work around the whole of the area. I've been down as far as Callington, and John has gone up to Brixham, we covered a fair distance, we went where the customers wanted us. John and I employed some contractors, carpenters, like Lasky Elliott down at Knap Mill, plumbers were Terry Hancock, his Father was over at Warcombe, painters who came along at the time, ironwork was done by Russell Baker, most professionally in my opinion. I built his

bungalow and I was building the entrance to it when my second set of twins were born in 1967.

Reg. You are jumping a bit now, because you were married to Connie?

Basil. I married Connie on the 25 March 1957 and we moved into the cottage where we are now. I bought it from Capt. Conran in 1952; Corner Cottage, but we call it Cosy Cot, just near the Church, it was the closest house to the Church but that is no longer the case, we lived here very happily. We had two sets of twins; they were seven years apart, one set born in 1960 and the other in 1967. All boys, all now tradesmen, electrician, carpet layer, painter and decorator and builder.

Reg. Footballers too?

Basil. Rugby players, I had never played rugby in my life, but I changed from soccer to rugby when they went to Kingsbridge. The instigator of that was Vic Ibbetson, down near the Chapel. I played football for Loddiswell when I was twelve in the first reserve game under the Captaincy of Bill Stone, he was living out at Kingston, his wife was Annie. He was Captain of the second team. Once we went over to Dittisham to play and we got a penalty in the first five minutes but we lost twelve to one. We soon improved, we won the Harvey Cup and we won the League in my playing time.

Reg. Did Loddiswell have two teams then?

Basil. Yes, one was in the South Hams League and the other was the South Hams Reserve League. It was run by an old man called Stapleton, Frank Stapleton that lived next to Little Reads, he had three daughters and he ran the football in those days. They used to have a meeting in the old bottom room at the Turk's Head, 'course it is all altered now, you wouldn't know it. They used to have their meeting there Monday nights and pick the teams. That was the total extent of the sport in those days.

Reg. I remember you were involved in the building trade when the Blackdown Rings were improved in 1990. You came up and built the walls, gate pillars and the pedestal on the top of the motte.

Basil. I was quite honoured to be asked to do it and I'm pleased you took photos of the building

Above: The directional indicator on Blackdown Rings. 1990

and dragging the inscription stone with a trolley and ropes up to the top of the motte for fixing on top of the pedestal. It was a piece of Marble which came from Merrivale out on Dartmoor and William and Triggs of Newton Abbot did the polishing and carved the directional signs on the surface. I had a few good weeks out there. The stone that has the plaque inside the kissing gate is of particular interest. We were looking for a stone at the time and I said, "Why don't we take that big one out of the ditch?", so we did that and stood it up and concreted it in. Then the English Heritage lady came, she made us feel about two inches high; she said we shouldn't have done it because of the historical value of the stone and we should not have disturbed it.

Reg. **I then asked her how the stone had got in**

Below: Rebuilding the stone wall, Blackdown Rings. 1990

the ditch and she said it has been there for all time and I said I think you ought to be aware that all the level areas of the Blackdown Rings were ploughed up in the Wartime to grow potatoes and cereals and these large stones were dug out of the soil and bulldozed in there, so she had no further complaint.

Basil. Yes, that's exactly what happened, she went away with her tail between her legs! I don't think the stone had any historic value, I think it was chucked out of the way, any rate we've made good use of 'em now, it will stay there for many years.

I didn't actually retire until the year before last, twelve months ago last April, I'd been ill before that, I was in hospital on and off for nearly two years with all sorts of ailments, but I was very lucky through my working life, I only lost two half days of illness. One was when I worked over to Idestone Farm and one was down at Hatch, at Sid Tolchard's. I've been very, very lucky, no accidents or anything like that. I still travel up and down to Reads Farm, I go quite regularly. I went down there when Edward Pethybridge came from Inver Research Farm at the top of North Pool. He bought Reads Farm and wanted block work done around a barn, so I started and he's been a brilliant customer. Now I help Donald since his Father died a few years ago. I've been down there ever since, very good customers and more than that they are very good friends. When my wife, Connie died with cancer I used to go down there a lot, I even used to go down there Christmas mornings and help to feed the sheep, it gave me something to do and they put up with me then and are still putting up with me now.

Reg. *Now Sheila is here with you!*

Basil. Yes, she came from Kernborough. I've known her for many, many years. She lived with her family in Chillington and worked for Social Services. She had four children and later moved into Kingsbridge. I had the two sets of twins when my wife died and it was nine years after Connie died that I got married again. I wanted to see the boys settled first. They are now living their own lives and Sheila is putting up with me.

Jack Hine

Jack sadly passed away on 1st April 2001 He worked tirelessly for the British Legion. In 1999 he was presented with a medal for more than 50 years of fund raising for the Earl Haig Poppy Appeal.

Reg. I've come to see Jack Hine at No 11 Fore Street, Loddiswell. I want to talk to him about his early life because at the moment we are intending to rebuild the Well in Well Street as a Millennium Project and I know Jack used to live near that Well.

Jack. Yes, I know it very well indeed; my Mother, Father and all the family were born there. My Mother used to go down to the Well to fetch the water and she would often do her washing down there. Every other day she used to wash all our clothes there in the cold water. There wasn't any tap water in the houses and then they put the mains tap outside Mr Watts's house, all the people around there used to get their water from the Well before the mains came, Mr Watts, Mrs Freeman and the Sopers. Charlie Freeman lived opposite our house on the lower side of the road before Wilf and Elsie Burman came there. My Father said the well water used to come from the well up in Courtledge where the pump used to be. Then to another well in Cyril Brooking's place at Hillside Cottage and then in Yalland's of Pointridge, the water used to come down through there. Some wells did go dry but that well in Well Street never went dry, sometimes very slowly in the summer but there was always water. In the winter there was always plenty of water.

Jack Hine was born in Well Street before electricity and indoor sanitation was installed. His Mother coped with a large family and did the washing at the well in cold water. Jack learnt his trade as a baker, which he successfully did until his retirement. The village held him in high esteem for his contribution to the work of village life. A memorial seat was erected in the Village Square in his memory.

Reg. You said you were born down there, which year was that, Jack?

Jack. 1919. All of us were born there, five boys and four girls; we were all brought up in Well Street. There was Sid, Stanley, Alphonso, Jim and me, that were the boys, the girls were Mary, Florrie, Queenie and Rose. There was a big bank outside in Well Street and there were two beautiful stones, long stones and we used to go out there to sit. There used to be a bit of ground on the higher side of the road where my Father had chickens, fowls and rabbits, tame rabbits and the barn there used to belong to Mrs Treeby, where Mr Wilf Paynter used to keep his horses and wagons. The houses on the lower side of the road, the terraced houses, had broken down, 'course they used to be thatched cottages, but we all lived in a thatched cottage in them days, and so did Mrs Burman and Charlie Watts, he was the thatcher, but the Sopers over the road they had slate.

When I went to Loddiswell School Mr Bryant

Above: Children in Well Street with Fred Keswick's thatched Blacksmith's shop in the background.

was the teacher, he taught me, and he had a son called Tony. He used to take us up to the allotments in Poor Man's field at Loddiswell Butts, all the allotments were up Loddiswell Butts on the Ham side and the School had eight or nine of them. We used to walk up with our tools on our shoulders.

Reg. **You've heard the story about the Widger boys at Cold harbour !**

Jack. Yes, Frank and Fred. One Friday night they decided there was no point in going back to school again so they hid behind the row of beans and the boys went off back to the school. Then they set off for home. When 'Boss' Bryant got back to the school he realised they were missing so he got on his motor bike and caught up with them at Fern Hill Cross. He said 'right boys you go back to school where you should be' and he followed them back on his bike. Then he said 'now you can go home'.

When I first went to Loddiswell School I did a milk round for Mrs Yalland of Pointridge, I used to go around with cans of milk to different people.

After Loddiswell I went to Kingsbridge School in 1932. I was one of the first pupils there when it was built, the big one, the Modern Secondary

School. I was thirteen years of age then, but I only went there for a month because I was coming 14 in August and then I left. I came back to the village to Mr. Ward's, Reg Ward of the London House Stores. I started going to Loddiswell Station to meet the first train for the papers, the Western Morning News which was one and a half pence. Then I delivered them all round the village, before I had a cup of tea at Mrs Ward's. Then I had to go down and meet the London train, the School train that the boys going to the Grammar School from Loddiswell caught. Owen Elliott, the Winzer boys, Jeff and Teddy Winzer and some boys who used to live up towards Brent. That was about a quarter to nine. Sydney Jeffery worked at Ward's for two years before me.

I was called up from Ward's in 1939 when war broke out. I had me papers to say I was called up, so I told Mr Ward I had to leave, he said 'I can get you off because you are a baker' I said 'no, I'd better go'.

I was living at Little Gate and then moved to Rose Cottage in Well Street, we went in there when Freddie Kernick moved up to Tyepitte Cottages. That was the house immediately above Pointridge. I went into the Army from there, that was before I was married. I went to Bulford, I was only there for two days, I didn't do any drill, I never seen a gun, never saw a rifle, then I went to Aldershot baking bread; they had a big bakery there with 20 draw pallets and I

Right: "I went into the Army ...I went to Bulford, I was only there for two days, I didn't do any drill, I never seen a gun, never saw a rifle, then I went to Aldershot baking bread."

was there for three years. That's where I met my wife Rose, she was a cook, she was in the Forces, she came from Kent, so I married her. I was there right through the war, I never got sent abroad or anything. Then I was posted to Wales baking bread for the Royal Marines and I stayed there until 1946. They were short of bakers and as I passed three exams I would get threepence, sixpence and ninepence extra on top of my army money for achieving them. It was very good because I went in with a trade; you get more money if you have a trade so I was very well off.

I got married in Maidstone and I said to my wife 'you'll find a difference between living in the town and the country'.

I brought her down here once for a holiday, I said 'I've got a job' and she agreed to stay. At that time they put up four prefabs in Oakwood Park and the Council gave me one, they gave Les Hine one and Jack Marsh one and a Schoolmaster, called Higman. Later Chris Ryder lived in one, then Wilf Lilley he lived in one. I lived up there for 20 years, and they were lovely, I couldn't understand why they didn't build concrete blocks around them. Later Christian Michell and Margaret Common, the schoolteachers, came there from the Terrace.

When I came back from my army service Mr. Ward's had closed. Then Owen and Bert returned from the Air Force and Mr and Mrs Gerry were at the end of their Lease. Owen said to me, "Jack what are you going to do, do you want to go back baking again?" I said, " Yes I've done it all my life" so I went to Elliott's Bakers Shop.

They were there for 30 years and I worked with them for 30 years. They delivered around the country with two vans. I had a little Morris van and there was a Ford van. I used to go out to California on Mondays and around Woodleigh and Moreleigh one day and we used to go Churchstow way Wednesday and Saturdays.

Bread was four pence in them days, that was for a two pound loaf. When we went out to Gara Bridge and up to Moreleigh, the Balls that lived at New House used to have four pound loaves, great big loaves, they had to last 'till we came

again. They had two daughters and four sons, 'course 'twas cheap in they days".

We had coal ovens, we used to get the coal from Westcotts, 'twas always fired and inside there was big flat stones and every year Tom Squires would come up on a Sunday and go inside that oven and check all the slabs. Every three years he would take 'em out and put new ones in for us because they were burnt. The coal fire was in under the stones; it used to go a long way back with the bricks on the top of it.

We had one big area to put the bread in, tuff cakes, buns etc. we used to make everything including cakes and sponges, great big sponge rolls. I used to start four o'clock in the morning and went on until I finished, sometimes I was early, sometimes I was late, about three o'clock in the afternoon. Sometimes I went out on the rounds in the afternoon with Owen, Bert would do one round, we would do the other.

When they sold the business to Mr Peter Nathan I worked for him and after five years he put it up for sale again. Geoff Lewis had a partnership with Geoff Collins, but he soon left and then John and Mary Pettitt bought it in 1987. I was baking right up until then and I was 67 when I finished.

Reg. But you still continued to do some work after that?

Jack. Yea. When Loddiswell built the toilets they asked me if I would clean them so I started to clean the toilets and the roads around Loddiswell to keep the village clean and tidy. I did that for many years but eventually I called it a day. I have had a very good life.

Left: Jack worked tirelessly for the British Legion. In 1999 he was presented with a medal for more than 50 years of fund raising for the Earl Haig Poppy Appeal. His contribution to the village community was marked by asking him to plant the Millennium oak tree on the Loddiswell Butts.

Cyril Brooking

Cyril developed leukaemia in his mid-70s and despite such a debilitating disease he fought back with his usual cheerfulness and courage. Sadly, he died in February 2003 and there could be no better memorial to him than his own life story

Reg. Cyril you've spent all your working life in Loddiswell?

Cyril. All my life actually except for the War years. I was born at Providence Place in 1923 and was there until I was six months old, then I went to Pear Tree Cottage in the Courtledge. I stayed there until I got married and came down into Hillside Cottage in 1953.

Reg. What do you remember about your young life in Loddiswell?

Cyril. We used to make our own pleasures, we had a very good life, we enjoyed it, we didn't know any different. If we went anywhere we had to go by pushbike or walk. I remember we had hoops that Uncle Sandover used to mend, he used to mend 'um for nothing and Freddie Kernick used to charge us a penny. Then we had trolley's which we made from old prams, and then I had an old pushbike, and Horace Camp, Snuffy Harris and me raced each other from the top of Terrace and down around here. I once hit the wall of this house and was hung up on the ledge. I cut my head open and I was unconscious for a week. We enjoyed life however and though we didn't have much we enjoyed what we had.

I went to Loddiswell School and when I was

His vivid memory of his early years and gratitude for the joy of simple pleasures portray his kindly disposition. The War Years, serving in the submarine service were a tremendous challenge, but his steadfast courage and strength of character helped him through those dangerous years. Throughout his life gardening has been his greatest pleasure.

eleven I went to the Secondary School in Kingsbridge. I used to walk down to the station to catch the train to go, that was before Jimmy Clark had a coach to take us. I was there for, maybe 18 months; it was nearly as well to walk to the school as to walk to the station. When I left school I went to work in the gardens at Coombe Royal and worked there until the early part of the war. Then I left and went down to the Concrete works and we went to build gun emplacements at Salcombe, Bolberry and Burgh Island. They were built looking this way to the harbour and not out to sea and at Hope Cove we built pillboxes.

Reg. I remember the ones at Salcombe down below the Bolt Head Hotel. There were two six-inch naval guns there and I remember seeing them being fired one night when we were in the Home Guard.

Cyril. I went down there helping to put them in, they broke all the windows, particularly the four-inch ack-ack, anti aircraft guns, which had a sharp crack, they would break windows for past-time.

Although we were under a reserved occupation, Horace Camp, Den Perring and myself went and volunteered for the Navy. I

Above: "There were three submarines, the Valiant, the Untamed and the Untiring......The Valliant went out on her trials and was lost, ...Untamed went down in fresh water and hit the bottom so that was a good start to my submarine career." 1942

wanted to go in as a Stoker, but they wouldn't accept me as a Stoker as I wasn't colour blind or anything, they wanted seaman. I was called up on the 18 February 1942 when I was eighteen and a half. I went down to the Raleigh and was down there for six weeks training. I then did six weeks training as a gunner before I came home on leave. When I went back I was transferred out to Yealmpton and they said I was a volunteer for the submarine service, me and another chap called Bowhay. I said, not me, he is, but I'm not because I always said I'd shoot myself if they put me in one of them things. Anyhow, I passed and he failed with his nerves.

From there I went up to the Dolphin, did my submarine training there and then went up to Blythe and did some more training. I went on to Rothesay and Dunoon and then I was sent down to Newcastle, down to Walkers Yard where they were building the submarines. There were three submarines, the Valiant, the Untamed and the Untiring. The Valliant went out on her trials and was lost, they only found her a couple of years ago, the Untamed went down off Campbeltown but we got away with it, we were all right. Untamed went down in fresh water and hit the bottom so that was a good start to my submarine career.

Reg. You were on submarines for a number of years!

Cyril. Yes, until the end of the War, we did not know where we were sailing, that was always a secret, We didn't know, but we finished up in the Mediterranean, having done a patrol up off Norway. Only when we left harbour was the Captain told in his confidential papers, which he had to open up to see where we were directed to patrol. I was a gun layer and had a three-inch gun mounted on the superstructure. Our boat was only between six and seven hundred tons and carried eight torpedoes. We saw plenty of action in the Mediterranean, we sank 14 ships and that was the second highest tonnage sinkers in the U Class. They were merchant ships and barges full of ammunition, one was going to Italy, another was full with troops and we sank both of them.

Reg. What happened to the troops?

Cyril. We didn't stop to look for them, we did a quick exit. We had a few depth charges thrown at us, in fact one trip we did we were up off Monte-Carlo and there was a boat tied up so the Skipper said "we'll have a go at that one" 'cus it was a sitting target. So we fired two torpedoes at it and we missed, we couldn't make it out so we went down to Malta to the base to see why we missed and the conning-tower had been shifted two degrees with the depth charges we'd received, so of course we were two degrees out. We readjusted the submarine and then came back into Maddalena in Sardinia.

Reg. I suppose you hit the Quayside instead?

Cyril. No, I think they went up on the sand actually, but the most frightening part, I always reckon was when we were going through the mine fields off the south coast of France, because you could dive when you were going through them and you could hear the scraping of the wires on the hull as you went along. The chap on the asdic would say, sharp left, sharp right, port, starboard and all that; you had to be wide-awake on that sort of job. We had some good times as well, it wasn't all bad.

Reg. There were a couple of times Cyril, when you were reported missing.

Cyril. Yes, I was missing twice. The first time was off Northern Italy, near Genoa where we sank a merchant ship and of course he had escorts, there they gave us a good old leathering with depth charges. The Upstart, which was in the next section to us, came back in port and said, "They couldn't get away with it, they are bound to be sunk." We were two or three days missing and we had a job to get back in again, the depth

Below: Cyril, on the left, loading ammunition in Holy Loch in the U.K. submarine force. 1943

charges had mucked up everything in the boat, but we eventually managed to find our way back again. Of course all the lighting had gone and we had to get the engines working again and the motors for the generators.

They damaged our boat but the sides they held out alright because it was pressured up to about 260 lbs so you could go down to 260 feet and that was about as deep as you could go, but we didn't know what depth we were at. A big problem was loosing the light but we had painted everything with luminous paint and we had emergency lights. The luminous paint would show it all up so you could see what you were doing because that was something we had trained for.

The next time we went to Toulon to see if the Germans were making a merchant ship into an aircraft carrier. We waiting until some merchant ships were coming, they told us they were coming and the booms would be open. They wanted us to go in and so we went in and they

put the booms across again, so we couldn't get out. We were there for 72 hours and of course we didn't have any air and couldn't start the engines up or anything like that. We had to be very careful what we were doing, so of course we were reported missing again. They knew we had gone and not returned, but then some other merchant ships were going out so we came out with them down under. It was in the daylight and when we got outside they had two, what they called new J boats and they could drop 110 depth charges in ten minutes. So the Skipper lined them up, we had four torpedoes and we hit one and sank it and the other one, his mate came chasing us, he certainly gave us a good leathering.

Reg. **When you were in Toulon Harbour you couldn't surface very well without being seen!**

Cyril. We had to dive all day and surface at night, you couldn't start up anything 'cus they would find us, they were always checking the harbour. So that was a narrow escape but we got away with it. We had a good run of success with enemy shipping.

On one patrol we went out, nobody knew where we were going when we left harbour, until the Skipper opened his sealed orders. He said we were going off the coast of Spain and France because Spain was helping the Germans but Spain reckoned they weren't. Nobody told us what was on but we had to be ready early in the morning when it was breaking dawn for action stations, 'cus these two ships were coming around a headland and the Skipper knew the exact time they were coming. He knew the exact distance they were away and everything was all worked out before we ever seen them. Before they sank they gave us a bit of leathering but it wasn't too bad 'cus we went straight through where we sunk 'em, we went right through the middle of them so they couldn't fire down on us. They were around four to 5,000 tons each, they were fair size boats and were carrying ammunitions to the Germans, they always said they weren't helping the Germans but of course they were.

Reg. **Of course the submarine was one of the most dangerous of ships in the wartime!**

Cyril. Yes, because you were always in the front line. When you left harbour there was nobody to protect you, nobody knew where you were going or what you were doing. We were lost until we came back, we had eight torpedoes and if you got rid of them early you could come back but if you had them after three weeks you might have to stay for another week, you could be out for a month. We only had 600 gallon of water so washing was out, you didn't wash or shave or nothing like that.

Reg. **The torpedoes were about a ton in weight?**

Cyril. Yes, they were about a ton in weight and you had to be careful in loading 'twas all done by the crew.

We had a crew of 34 or 35 with the officers and everybody. There wasn't a lot of room. If you slept on the lockers, when you got out somebody else would get in, it was as simple as that. A lot of the time you didn't sleep at all 'cus you were in action stations. Yes, 'twas quite enjoyable, there were good times as well as the bad ones but we had our fair share of both.

Reg. **Did you find the conditions were rather claustrophobic?**

Cyril. No, I didn't, I thought I might, 'course you couldn't wash or nothing like that, when you went to sea you might be going to sea for a month and with only 600 gallon of water to start with when you left harbour, you couldn't make water or air so you had to look after that. Perhaps you could have a bucket once a week and then you would all have to swill off or something like that out of the same bucket.

Just for a few days we would have fresh food but when that was all gone you were on tinned rations and then on dehydrated rations. You had to be on duty two hours and four off, of course, there would be actions stations so after two hours you may be on for perhaps another four hours. Then, of course, it was your turn to go back on duty again, so sometimes you were on for eight hours or longer.

Reg. **When you were off duty how did you pass the time away?**

Cyril. You had to sleep because you weren't allowed to use up the oxygen, as we weren't making any when we were submerged. We dived at dawn to charge our batteries so you had to look after what you had. There were no games except when we were on the surface, then we might play the odd ludo or crib, there wasn't anything else you could do; "twas a rough old life but when we came ashore you made up for it.

When I was demobbed it was quite a change, it was a big difference. It was July 1946 and I went down on the railway line then. I worked down there for three and a half years and after that I went to Torr Quarry where I stayed until I retired through ill health at 61.

Reg. Did you suffer any ill effects from the war?

Cyril. Not really, I've got a bit hard of hearing because when you surfaced, the pressure in the boat used to pull on your ears but other that, no, I think I got away with it.

Of course my Father suffered from gas in the First World War, he was gassed and the British Legion was still fighting for a pension for him when he died. He made the best of life, he loved his bees and he loved his garden, but he couldn't do a lot, we always helped him and that interested me. My old Grandfather was a gardener so I suppose it was in the blood somewhere along the line.

Reg. Grandfather Sandover?

Cyril. No, Turpin, Mother's Father, he was a gardener up at a big place at Bovey Tracey. I think it is National Trust now.

I loved gardening too, used to get up at half past four in the morning and go gardening, back and have my breakfast and off again. I loved it, not only to supply the household but I loved showing, Loddiswell Show, Kingsbridge, Stokenham, Plympton, Plymouth, I showed all over the place, once it gets in your blood you enjoy it.

When I was 70 I won two cups in Kingsbridge and they said 'hope to see you again next year'. I said 'no you won't, I've finished, I have retired at the top so I've finished'. I won one outright, the other I won for that year.

I did the gardening for Bert Taylor and we won the cup in Kingsbridge six years running and then for another three, in fact we had it for

Above: Receiving the Gardening Cup from President Rita Greig, Loddiswell Show,

nine years.

Reg. You said you spent some time down at the Sandover's, the wheelwright!

Cyril. I remember seeing him put the old iron band onto a wagon wheel outside in the orchard. It was red hot and carried out with tongs and dropped onto the rim of the wooden wheel. Buckets of water were then thrown over it so it contracted on to the wheel and didn't burn it. We used to go back there to see them and if Mum and Dad were in hospital we used to go over there to live. We had our meals there and if we were having our dinner and left any you would have to eat it for tea; my Auntie wasn't allowed to throw it away. We weren't allowed to speak at the table and we used to grumble in our own minds but we weren't at home and really they were as good as gold.

We all provided our own entertainment back in them days. If you wanted to go to Plymouth you had to go down and catch the train at half past seven, you would go up to Brent and then catch the train down to Plymouth. You were down there for about two hours and then you had to come home, it took you all day and you wouldn't get home 'till half past seven at night. It was very difficult getting around in them days. I am lucky to be able to sit here in the sun lounge at Hillside Cottage, overlooking the church, my garden and lawn and there are, as you see, still roses around now in October.

Fred and Evelyn Brooking

Less than twelve months after this interview Fred passed away on 24 September 2000. He experienced great changes during this lifetime but adjusted to them with good humour and contentment.

Reg. This morning I have come to visit Fred Brooking and Evelyn, or Eve as Fred calls her, they live just opposite the Congregational Church in Arundell Place. I would like to talk to you about your early life. Were you born in Loddiswell Fred?

Fred. I was born in Town's Lane in 1906, up in those houses where the bungalows are now, just before Town's Park and I went to school from there. What do I remember about my school days? Oh, I don't know, Parker was there when I first went down there, he was the school master of Loddiswell British School.

'Course the other Church School was going then and Sydney Scoble was the headmaster up there, he later lived down at Chevithorne.

I spent all my school days at Loddiswell and I left when I was thirteen. In those days we didn't come out until four o'clock, I don't know what we did after school. My Father worked on the farm and he only had one day a year off, Good Friday, and we always had to go gardening, that was about all the days off he had in them days. When I left school I went down with Sam Scobell who lived at Cross Farm before he went out to Reveton, he was the Father of Leonard Scobell. Sam Scobell went in after the

Fred was part of a large family growing up with many siblings; he quickly learnt to give and take and this has stood him in good stead throughout his happy marriage. His life's work has revolved around the parish and his memories of drawing stone from the local quarries for building and road making gives an insight into the beginnings of our present road structure

Hannafords who moved over to Sigdon. My main job was driving horses, working out in the fields. When we were at Reveton we grew corn and I remember threshing days. They used to come around with the threshing tackle, I can't remember who came before Jack Baker. I stayed at Reveton a couple of years and then I went to Ham Farm, my brother George was down there at that time, but I didn't stop anywhere for very long, then I went with Tom Rundle driving horses. He and Jack Hyne were hauling stone for the roads. I used to draw from Idestone quarry and I remember you boys at Yanston Farm, you were about seven, eight year old.

Reg. Was the stone blasted out ?

Fred. They ripped it out in they days with picks and iron bars, no blasting down there, and as they ripped it out I had to load the cart.

I think I had a horse called Lion and would stop talking to you and your brother at Higher Yanston Farm as we went by, the horse would go on and then I had to run to catch up to him.

'Course there wasn't any traffic about in those days. I had to take it to the Council tips, it was big stone and men were at the tips to break it up, Harry Soper and Tommy Luscombe's boy Ern

Top: Award winning gangers, 1959. Left to right. Fred Brooking, Peter Carpenter, Gilbert Garland, Harold Fice, Harold Reeves.

Bottom: Gangers on the Kingsbridge to Brent railway line. 1959

Luscombe, they all went breaking stone. They wore leather gloves and broke the stone down to about the size of an egg with a hammer. The stone was used for surfacing the roads in Loddiswell and part of Aveton Gifford parish. Jack Hyne and Tom Rundle used to work together but I worked for Tom Rundle, that was before Jack Hyne had a lorry in 1929. Jack Hyne used to keep his horses and cart down where the Chapel Hall is, before it was rebuilt in 1930. Tom Rundle kept his at Cross Farm and we had to go up cutting chaff for the horses, it was hand operated, so it meant turning the old handle.

Then lorries took over hauling stone so I went down to Rake Quarry when I was 21 and was there until I was 40. I was there until the War and then I had to go up to Paignton to the Gas Works. I was up there for about four years and was only cleaning up, 'twas a waste of time really. I was there until the end of the War and then I came back and got married to Evelyn who lived at Greystones, that was on the 12 February 1945.

Her Father was George Brooking who went in the Navy but he was too old to go to sea. He was in a section of the Royal Naval Fire Brigade in Plymouth and died while still in the Service as a result of smoke inhalation during the bombing. I could have gone back to Torr quarry after the War but I decided to work on the railway and I was there for 14 years. When the railway closed in 1963 I went back to Torr again until I retired in 1971.

Reg. **Who was working with you then?**

Fred. I was on the permanent way with Phil Lakeman, Gilbert Garland, Harold Reeves from Kingsbridge and Horace Fice. I was living then up Chapel Lane next to Gilbert Garland until this house in Arundell Place was built in 1968. Here 'tis a glorious house in a good position, Pillars of Dartmouth built it and made a good job of it.

We used to go badger digging Saturday afternoons, down Leigh, Chantry, Idestone, Yabbacombe and the Brakes at Great Gate, there were badgers all the way around.

Reg. **You have a nice garden, who does all the work ?**

Fred. I do all the back garden but they won't allow me out on the front lawn where it is steep, but I always did up the back garden, not bad for a 93-year-old.

Reg. **Evelyn, you have lived here since 1968 and before you were married at Greystones with your parents George and Rosina Brooking who farmed there!**

Evelyn. Yes, he farmed at Greystones and then my brother Cyril took on the farm, you call him Cyril and I call him Cyril, because that is what he was called at school, but everyone else called him Sid. One of the family did that too, it is something like Rodney, in his school days they called him Charlie. When his future wife Diane went out with him she thought he was called Charlie and it was only later that she discovered he was called Rodney. People used to say 'Come here Charlie' and it stuck to him. It's all wrong really, you mustn't do that. I've got a great grandson and I sometimes say 'Come here rascal' and he says 'don't call me that Gran, say Jack', he puts me in my place.

Reg. **When I was at Loddiswell School you were living at No. 1 Council houses. I used to go out the back gate of the school, across New Road and in to have a biscuit with Cyril and your Mum and then we would slip back to school when the bell rang.**

Evelyn. Oh, you crafty boys !

Fred. When the Council houses were built in about 1927/28 we drew the stone for the foundations. We drew the stones there and over at the Churchyard at the same time for building the wall at the new Churchyard which was taken out from the Court House field, and the wall had to be built up to contain it. There was a man called Rogers from Aveton Gifford who built it. We used to draw for a day from Rake quarry, down where Russell Baker had his workshop, for the Churchyard wall, and the next day from Loddiswell quarry for the new houses.

Reg. **Your eldest sister was Georgette !**

Evelyn. Well, Bill was the oldest, he worked on the roads, then Tom who worked at the World's Stores in Kingsbridge. Jack Stear drove a little van around to the farms once a month and took the orders and then delivered a few days later.

Jack Stear was Gillian Stear's father. Later my brother Tom, worked at the London House stores here in Loddiswell.

Next came Georgette, she used to help your Mother at Yanston for a short time before Marjorie, who was with you for many years before she was called up for War Service. I came after Georgette and Roy was next. He went in the Army and when he came out he worked for Powlesland at Torcross, Mr and Mrs Powlesland kept the London House stores here before moving to Torcross. Next came Sid, he was working on the farm at Greystones because Father was in the Navy. Then came Myrtle and the youngest is Connie who was six years younger.

Myrtle worked for Major and Mrs Rainey and moved from Wood Barton with them up to Norfolk. She was up there for many years before she got rheumatoid arthritis. Mrs Rainey thought it was time for her to come home with her family as she was getting worse. She said she liked it up there and got to know the people, she was very happy working for them. When she was working at Wood Barton she used to go up in the Monastery where they used to keep chicken, that was after the War. Connie lived over at Woodleigh and married Ken Shute.

Reg. **You lived near 'Squire' Eastley!**

Fred. I always used to call him 'Squire' but one day someone said 'Hello Squire' and he shouted. 'No bucker me! I'm only plain Jack Eastley, I'm not Squire.'

Below: A couple outside the house in Town's Lane, Loddiswell, where Fred was born.

Bert Walke

Tape recording made in 1986

He lived in Loddiswell parish all his life until 1996 when he moved to Quay Court Nursing Home where he died at the age of 100 years and five days.

$\mathcal{B}$*ert.* I was born on 11 August 1896 at Lower Hazelwood, which was under a tenancy from Admiral Parker from Delamore, Cornwood, because Grandfather also rented a farm under the estate at Houndal, Cornwood. I remember the old Admiral, he was crippled up, he used to have a leather seat stitched on his breeches and they used to pull him down over the brake when he came there shooting. He used to shoot; they normally came about twice a year from Delamore.

I went to Loddiswell British School with my older brother Walter on a pony and we tied up in the stable at Great Gate Farm. When my brother Walter left Loddiswell School I had to take my younger brother Cyril on the pony. Sometimes if we didn't want to go to school we would find a stream and give each other a good soaking. We would return home and say there was torrential rain and we got soaked. Mother eventually became suspicious and we both had a good hiding! So we didn't try it again.

We liked it at home on the farm but Mother thought there ought to be a little culture in the family and arranged for me to take up violin lessons in Modbury. It was quite a performance getting me on the pony with the violin because

The village would have been poorer without his philosophy on all aspects of life. No matter what the question there was always a ready answer with advise on putting it right. His love of fishing started as a boy on the river Avon at Hazelwood and continued throughout his life. He could be infuriating but there was always a twinkle in his eye.

I didn't really want to go.

When we were at Hazelwood farmers used to bring their bulls and 'stop over' until the following morning and catch the train at Gara Bridge to take them to the Totnes Bull Sale. I remember two bulls called Dendeno and Macbeth, they were 32 cwt each, they were a mass of beef. The farmers brought a load of mangolds and bundles of hay and we would stop them there and their men. They would sleep there and then take them down to catch the train the next morning.

Farmer Helmer he brought a cow and a calf one night and left the man there and took them up by train, but they had to weigh the calf separately, he had to go in the Guard's van, he was two cwt and Father bought it and kept it for a bull. That was the one that attacked Peter Rundle that time, it was a wonder he wasn't killed, but Bessie Reeves, who helped my Mother at Hazelwood went out and drove the bull off. The boy had teased it and the bull turned on him, he started running and the bull chased him and got him down in a drain but with the brambles out over the drain the bull couldn't kneel on him, he was down out of the way. He was badly injured, broke his arm and the bull put his horn through his shoulder, he was knocked up pretty badly. T'was a pity, we didn't have the benefit of that bull. The cow she made 28 guineas, which was a big price at that time, beautiful great cow, back straight the tail fitted in.

Now, why can't I get a cwt of muriate of potash? I always used to be able to go in and buy a cwt, but the merchants won't let me have it now, they want you to buy their compounds and they don't balance it right. I got too much nitrogen already, everything grows up leaves and I get little cabbage, full of leaves and I want savoys solid. Down at South Devon Farmers I can get a ten-ton load but what would I do with a ten-ton load in my little orchard.

I left Hazelwood and went into the butchery business on The Bank in Loddiswell in 1927 when I was married and our two sons were born above the butcher's shop.

When I was coming back the other day I looked into see Sydney Hobbs at South Brent, he had a beautiful bullock there hanging up, there wasn't any waste fat on 'un, a little more would have suited me, but there wasn't any old grain, it broke up so easily there wasn't that old muscle there. Mr. Hobbs told me the price of beef was much firmer, he had to pay a fair bit more for this bullock.

Reg. Beef prices have been very poor!

Bert. You people may think so but us fellows that got to buy it don't think so.

Reg. I think it's the cost of rearing them.

Bert. Now, what has happened to all these 150,000 tons of beef that they put it cold storage three years ago when there was a surplus. It's still in cold storage, I've never heard of it being taken out.

They have had the cost of keeping it there, the shrinkage when it comes out and it's got to come out as frozen beef. If they had sold it cheap to the butchers and paid a subsidy to the farmers the public would have eaten it. The butcher would have been cutting up decent joints, now he cuts a joint the size of that cup for the weekend and the rest of the week they live out of tins. That's what's happening, I see it!

It would have been better for the farmer; he

Above: The first shot at Hazelwood, 1914
Everyone in the village called him 'Butcher' because of his trade and that name stayed with him after he retired in 1966 at the age of 70.

would have got his price with the subsidy, like when he had 69 shillings and six-pence cwt subsidy back in the 1960s. I could buy a bullock for £40 less then and I sold three bullocks a week, 26 lambs a week and nine to eleven pigs a week. People were eating some meat then. As the subsidy came down and the price rose I hit the time when I lost 800 quid!

There was no subsidy, I was paying about £124 a bullock then and I woke up and put my beef prices up. I didn't make anything but I held my own and I went down to a bullock and a half a week, it stopped just like that.

We had all this surplus beef in Australia, there was somewhere about two million bullocks shot and buried, you know it's fantastic, they shot all those bullocks. They went out on the ranges and shot them, the Government paid them so much a head to do it because of the surplus. That didn't ought to be with some of the world starving.

Now I see there's a job with the French, they've slapped a levy on our English lambs, 43 pence a pound, which is more than the price of the French produced lamb. We should eat our own meat, not buy this rubbish we are having from them.

Now you got the Limousine, I hate the sight of

them. I've seen their bulls, they've got an enormous neck on 'um, long, and the leg tapers away and the muscle don't show until two-thirds of the way up to the pin. It isn't more than good stewing beef, and they are crying them up, they go abroad and shout what a wonderful breed this is. The man that brings them in, he gets a bit of money out of it, but what about us poor devils.

The same with the Landrace pigs, they brought them in from Sweden at £1,000 a time, this is the breed they said but we didn't buy the real Landrace from Denmark; they were not allowed to sell them. We had an inferior Landrace, but there is always the flyboy, the smart guy who sees how to make money. We've got better breeds in this country.

This country has been disarming with this Labour Government, they cut everything down, they've ruined us and now we've got a job to pull out of it, I don't know if it's too late. Us have

Below: "I...went into the butchery business on The Bank in Loddiswell in 1927 when I was married, and our two sons were born above the butcher's shop." 1938

got a million and a half unemployed running around, I don't know where it will finish.

You see we stopped buying all the good meat; we used to get some beautiful stuff. I could get New Zealand lamb in season, I could get South African beef and Argentine beef second to none, rare young beef, proper little tubs, Aberdeen Angus. I could buy legs of beef there five pence a pound better than our own, tender. Then we had Canadian lamb, Icelandic lamb. They would start coming through in a different season; of course our English would only last so long. I would run Canterbury (New Zealand) until the English came in, then I would run both until I started to cut down on the Canterbury and bring up the English, they would go on until October when I found they were getting tougher. If they weren't ready by October they were bad doers and by Christmas they would eat like leather.

Now we are not allowed to buy anything except what comes out of the Common Market, they send us a lot of rubbish and we take it like lambs! If I was farming now I'd have the good old South Devon, you've got the beef and you've got the milk, us should have plenty of milk. Now we have overdone it, us got a surplus of milk, a surplus of powdered milk, us have got a surplus of everything bar money, us be in a bad state!

Bert Walke was not called up in the First World War as he was a farmer in a reserved occupation and was exempt. In the Second War he was a sergeant in the Special Constabulary. He served in this for 20 years from November 1935 to March 1956.

He was a very keen fisherman; he used to fish the River Avon and in later years owned various boats, fishing off East Portlemouth and Bantham. The largest fish he caught was a diver off Thurlestone who surfaced in a rage with the fishhook firmly established in the rear of his wet- suit!

He only sold his boat when he was 91 years of age and until that time he was still driving his car.

Below: Fishing at the mouth of the Avon. 1967

Frank Carpenter

Frank and Margaret, his wife, shared many outside interests together. Margaret was suddenly taken ill and after many months of nursing care she passed away in June 2002.

*R*eg. *Frank and Margaret Carpenter live at Virginia Cottage and Frank is going to talk about his experiences throughout his life.*
Frank. I lived at a place called Worcester Park in Surrey. When I was seven we had a dairy at the top of our road called Joe's Dairy and I got a job there as a milk boy, working at week-ends and holidays delivering milk around.

The war started in September 1939 when I was eight, and when we were out and the sirens went people used to say, "Come into the air-raid shelter." Sometimes you could be there for an hour before the all-clear went, this made us later and later on the milk round. These were Anderson shelters, buried in the garden, or there were tabletops that are Morrison Shelters, they were indoors. Many people just had cupboards under the stairs and you would go in there and sit with the people but because it made us so late very often we would carry on with the rounds. If we heard a bomb coming we just lay down on the pavement. I had one or two narrow escapes, we were in a cul-de-sac and a bomb dropped around the corner and because of the angle of the blast, the milk truck wobbled but we were

Memories of his early years are very vivid to Frank. When he was seven he got a job at Joe's dairy in Worcester Road, Surrey delivering milk in a hand drawn cart during the time of the 'buzz' bombing of London when he had a few narrow escapes. His first introduction to Loddiswell was in the war years visiting his sister, Ruth, an evacuee. After National Service in the RAF the family returned to Loddiswell in 1951 and quickly settled into village life.

all right, we were laid down. The truck was a three wheeler which we pushed along, we did two roads and then went back and filled up to do another two.

By the time I was ten I started with a horse and cart at United Dairies, I liked the horses and used to go into the stables and help look after the horses, that was the milkman's job to look after his horses. The horses knew their rounds and would stop at the right houses and then go on to the next one and stop, it was very convenient.

We had lost our Mother in 1943. It wasn't through the war but she died of cancer. It was only my sister and myself left at home. Ruth was evacuated down here and I came down on holiday and liked it here. She was evacuated because of the buzz bombs and as it was so bad the schools were closed, as it was too risky to have too many children in one place.

We used to meet for two hours a week in someone's house in the same street as we lived in and the teacher came there to give us our lessons; I came down on holiday with Father in 1944. Father was glad to leave me here while he was working and I was left on my own during the day.

I left school at 14, which was general in those days. After the war I did go back and work in the signal box at Waterloo Station. We had a Station Master's office where three of us worked; I was what you call a booking lad in the signal box. I came down on holiday again, we used to catch the 10.50 pm. train and as I was waiting for the train a man asked me where I was going and I replied "a little old place down in Devon called Loddiswell." He asked if I knew Mr and Mrs Garland as he was evacuated there in the early part of the war. His name was George Tier. I did four years in the signal box, it was the first electrical signal box, the signal levels were only about six inches high. On the way home after night duty at about 6 am I went into the signal box at my home station where they had the great big signal levers.

Reg. Did you have to do National Service?

Frank. Yes. I had two years in the R. A.F. 1949 to 1951. I was called up at 18 and posted to Calne in Wiltshire at a place called Yatesbury. I was a cook and butcher, learning a trade! In 1951 when I came out I went back on the railway and twelve months later we moved down here.

Reg. Did you continue on the railway?

Frank. They said they had transfers for us, my Father, Peter and myself. My brother Peter was all right, he got a job on the local Kingsbridge line, but the only jobs for my Father and I were in Plymouth which was a long way to go as in those days all we had were push bikes. I did a couple of labouring jobs and then, under a Government Scheme, went on a farm to learn about farming at a place called Cranleigh in Surrey. I did five years there learning all branches of farming. I enjoyed doing that as when I was evacuated down here I used to help down at Greystone with Sid Brooking, in those days with horses and carts. I left Cranleigh in 1958 and went to work at Wizaller for Mrs Goss and then to Brownstone for Johnnie Sluggett before he moved to Rake Farm.

I left farming in 1961 and went to work for the South West Electricity Board (SWEB) until I retired in 1991. I did 30 years but I had to retire early.

Above: The RAF Catering Corps. 1950. Frank stands on the left. "I was a cook and butcher, learning a trade!"

Reg. You were working on the main distribution lines.

Frank. Yes, We started by making up a gang of fourteen to take all the electric into farms. When we started it was pick and shovel, we put the poles up, it had to be all done by hand. In fact we took electricity into Widecome in the Moor. We even took it out to your place at Lilwell and did a good bit out there.

Reg. Were you involved in connecting the lines?

Frank. Yes, I started off as labourer and then lineman's mate in 1966. I went on a course in 1969-70 on what they call 'live-line' and that was working on the overhead alive, 11,000 volts. I did that for about three years and then became an ordinary linesman, working on overhead cables, low and high voltage.

Reg. How does live-line work? Is everything done with insulated poles?

Frank. We have insulated poles, tested to 75,000 volts per foot. We have a code of practice that you have to work by and then everything is OK. We had one or two faults with cracked insulators but we didn't have any serious faults. It was safe as houses, you might say, that is if you did it right and not cut corners.

I retired before I was 65 because I had angina. I went and had an operation but luckily I did not need a by-pass, they put balloons up my arteries and stretched them.

Reg. In retirement you have been able to do

other things!

Frank. Yes, I took up bowling; we do short mat and outdoor green bowling. Half a dozen of us got together and decided we would like to form a club for short mat bowling in the Village Hall. We were able to get enough money to buy one mat, and then we begged and borrowed and got another one.

We have a membership of 26 to 28 members and are doing very well in it. It is surprising how many villages around have short mat bowling. Loddiswell has done very well in competitions, we have been top of the League twice, we were top of the Second Division one year and we took the Knockout League as well.

The next year we were promoted to the First Division and we went right through and took the First Division Trophy. We were runner-up in the Knockout Competition, so we had a very good team, a good lot of local village people in it, all ages.

Reg. **Margaret is here listening to us, how did she become involved?**

Frank. Well, I was a Member of St. John's Ambulance and Margaret became a nurse in it, and having shared a few duties we decided to get together.

Reg . **As simple as that?**

Frank. That was 24 years ago when we first met. I have given up St John's Ambulance as we had to decide whether we would do that or bowling which we both enjoyed and there wasn't time to do both.

Below: Short mat bowling at Kingsbridge Sports Centre. 2000

Hilda Harvey

Reg. **This morning I have come to see Hilda Harvey of No 2. Ashwood Park. Were you born in Loddiswell Hilda?**

Hilda. I was born in Churchstow at Coax Cottage at the bottom of the village in 1920 and then when I was five my parents took a sweet shop, petrol pump and post office up in the village. My Dad used to cycle off to Plymouth with his rabbits and return with a joint of beef, which he bought for six shillings. At eleven years old I won a scholarship to Totnes, two years later my parents went to live at Newton Ferrers for a couple of years. The land in that area did not suit my Father's health so we came to live in Loddiswell at No 2. The Bank in 1936, just before the time of the Coronation of George VI. We had celebrated the Silver Jubilee of George V at Newton Ferrers.

Reg. **What do you remember about the Coronation?**

Hilda. All the houses were beautifully decorated and there was a big arch from Elliott's Stores across to Phoenix Place. We had fancy dress and food in the Chapel Hall and the Sports over in the Courtledge. The weather was lovely. I taught in the Church Sunday School in the days of the Rev. George and Mrs Bliss. When I left school in

Hilda's involvement with the School, Church, Women's Institute and Over Sixties Club has given her a mental stimulation to participate in the thriving activities of our community. She has recorded events at the school and village weddings since 1966. Gardening has been one of her great joys and poetry another. Her poetic skills have been recognised in her poems about village life.

1937 I went to Bristol and worked in the Church of England's Children's Waifs and Strays home at Wick House to train as a Nanny. My first ambition was to be a music teacher, but music was not encouraged at schools in those days and I was not allowed to continue learning. I was there two years and then returned to Wrangaton as a nanny for the Lobb family, Jane Rogers at Hendham, her sister and a relative who was an evacuee at that time.

When I left I went to Moorhaven and stayed there until I had to return to look after my Mother who was not very well. I met Raymond when I was working as a nanny and he was working for J Coaker, the butchers at Moorhaven as well as sometimes on the farm. Raymond and I were married at Loddiswell Church on the 29th of May 1943 and I continued with the post round on a bicycle in the Hazelwood area; there were four rounds in the parish. When I dropped that I did all the post rounds in the village.

Raymond was posted overseas in August in 1943 and when he went I worked at the South Hams Packing Station for a while before I went back to nursing, assistant nurse at Kingsbridge until

Raymond came home. He had been a paratrooper, he joined the Infantry but as they wanted paratroopers he joined them. He really wanted to fly but unfortunately he had not studied algebra so he didn't get through, he had about 80 odd jumps. He trained at Ringmere, Manchester and then was posted to Africa and he came from there to Italy with several other volunteers as the Allies pushed up through the country.

Eventually he was selected to return to the U.K. to train as an Officer as he wished to make the Army his career, but in the meantime I had a letter to say that he was missing, wounded, presumed a Prisoner of War. I was still doing the post round at that time and I had never done it so fast as that day. I didn't hear any thing for six weeks.

Just before our wedding anniversary I had a letter from the War Office to confirm that he was wounded and a prisoner of war. He was dropped behind the enemy lines in Italy and was captured. I was worried because he said if he was wounded he did not wish to come home and be a trouble. He was wounded in the arms, but he changed his mind as he could survive. He was only a Prisoner Of War for ten months before he was repatriated. He had been shot in both arms and had a bullet in his chest. People remember him wearing black gloves, as he did

Below: Decorated arch in Fore Street on King George 6th Coronation. 1936

not like people to see his hands and arms.

The following year Colin was born, we were still living with Mum on The Bank but in 1947 we were allotted this house, No 2 Ashwood Park. I have lived here ever since and I am the last original tenant since the houses were built, that is 55 years. In 1955 I helped Mrs Hart at the School before going to Courtlands, the guesthouse, to help Mrs Powell. In 1964 her family had grown up and I took the post at Loddiswell School as Cook/Supervisor. I was there from 1964 to 1983 and then two years with the Play School. That was the end of my working days.

Reg. Your Father, Alphaeus Ball, was a rabbit trapper until Myxomatosis killed them off in 1954.

Hilda. Yes. He used to sell them to Tonkins in Kingsbridge and he also used to cycle to Plymouth on an old Post Office bike, with them hanging from the carrier on the front and over the cross bar. I always remember when Father was coming home on his bike one day Doris Pile was walking home and Father stopped and

Below: Hilda had great poetic skills and this is a poem she wrote about her time at school.

Farewell with a Plateful of Memories.

Nineteen years have I been Cook-in-Charge,
I've fed the small, the medium and the large,
Most have eaten everything with ease,
There have been a few so hard to please,
But several thousand meals I have prepared
And many, many hours have I shared
With Loddiswell School.

Changes have occurred throughout the years,
Some brought laughter and some brought tears,
But generally speaking I have enjoyed the work
Challenges I have never tried to shirk.
For several thousand meals I have prepared
And many, many hours have I shared
With Loddiswell School.

asked her if she would like a lift. She said 'yes', so she rode from Sorley Cross down to the bridge on the cross bar with Father on the bike. He was up to all sorts of things like that.

Reg. I remember how he moved around his traps with the donkey and heavy wooden panniers on its back. He would go around the fields to set the traps and next morning, pick up the rabbits with it.

Hilda. When we first came to Loddiswell there wasn't a lot of traffic and we used to play ball out with the boys, I was a bit of a tomboy. We used to

Above: Hilda and Paratrooper Raymond Harvey, 1943. "…I met Raymond when I was working as a nanny…Raymond used to sing and whistle, you could hear him a long way off."

Right: My Father, Alphaeus Ball with his donkey, 1944

tie a rope to the railings of The Bank and they would get me to skip.

When we had a rounders match I was nearly always picked first as I could run fast. At Loddiswell Show before the war I was often anchorman in the tug-of-war team. I used to race against Evie Flint and they allowed us to go in the men's high jump; I once came fourth against the men. Evie Flint lived down at Leigh and her son is Richard Branston.

Since I retired I have been able to participate in various things in the village.

When I came here at the age of 15 I felt I belonged here. It took Raymond a little longer, being Welsh; he came from Bargoed, near Abergavenny.

When his Father and Mother came down here with him, his younger brother and his two sisters found work at Moorhaven and that is where I met him. Raymond used to sing and whistle, you could hear him a long way off.

Reg. **He had a good voice!**

Hilda. When he came home they arranged a concert and got him to sing, he sang, 'There'll always be an England.' I remember all the children standing round him.

I have recorded many of our village events as an amateur photographer; I recorded all the events at the School and village weddings and have kept scrapbooks since 1966, which concerned Loddiswell and my family.

I have now taken up quilling, it is done with strips of rolled paper gathered into flutings and I am able to use them to decorate cards for birthdays and other anniversaries.

Reg. **We have not said much about your family?**

Hilda. Colin was born at No 2 The Bank in 1946 and in August 1947 we moved up here and Trevor was born in October 1947. Felicity was born in May 1949; Beverley in 1951 but sadly only lived 17 days, Nigel was born in 1952.

I was always proud that the three boys were in each of the Services. Colin went into the Royal Navy and ended up as a Petty Officer having travelled the World. Trevor joined the Royal Air Force and finished as a Sergeant and now lives in Gloucester.

Felicity was a nanny at first and when she got married, joined the Services and became a Civil Servant; sadly she died two years ago. Nigel joined the Medical Corps and was a Staff Sergeant and now lives in Loddiswell.

It was my 80th birthday last year and we had a family reunion, when all the family came back. I love my garden and have entered into the Loddiswell Show Best Gardens Competition. I think I have won the cup on and off for about 15 years and I won it again last year.

Below: Hilda in her prize winning garden, 1996. "I love my garden and have entered into the Loddiswell Show Best Gardens Competition. I think I have won the cup on and off for about 15 years ..."

Sir William and Lady Lucy Peek

Sir William and Lady Peek live near Hazelwood House and the estate from which they retired in 1988.

Bill. I was born in London in 1919 and very shortly after I was born I lived in Hampshire in a bungalow with my Mother as my Father was still a serving soldier and was, in fact in Germany.

He had inherited Hazelwood before the First World War in 1910, purely by the coincidence that he was my Grandfather's second son. The eldest son would inherit Rousden in East Devon, a big house that my Great-grandfather had built, but my Father inherited Hazelwood. When Richard Peek died in 1857, he was a bachelor and none of his brothers were interested because they were London based tea merchants. They had no interest in a small country property as it then was, at Hazelwood, which consisted of two farms, Crannacombe next door and Higher Hazelwood, both of them a little over a hundred acres I suppose; both were dairy farms and both were tenanted.

My Father continued what had been the family policy of adding bits on to

After the First World War the large houses of the parish were still able to maintain their grandeur and lifestyle, Bill reminds us of those days. The normal vocation for the occupants was to join one of His Majesty's Services, and sons often followed in the chosen family regiment. During the Wars enormous sacrifices in human life were made. Bill lost his Father and only brother and Lucy both her brothers while serving their Country. The family went on to make beneficial contributions to the community. Bill Peek was appointed High Sheriff of Devon in 1972, and later the titles of Sir William and Lady Peek were inherited from his Uncle.

Hazelwood House and the only way you could add to Hazelwood is at the two ends because of the slope of the hill. My Father when he inherited Hazelwood firstly built on a new kitchen and another part of the house. He installed electric light. 110 volts, which was extremely unusual in those days, I believe the normal thing was 50 volts.

It had enormous glass batteries, generated by a single cylinder Petter paraffin engine that drove an enormous dynamo and that engine continued to provide electric light into the 1930s.

Then came the First World War, by then my Father was already a regular soldier and he went very early in the war with his regiment and was captured by the Germans at the first battle of Mons, that was the last lance charge between the Germans and the English. He was unfortunately knocked off his horse and captured and he spent the rest of the war in a Prisoner Of War (POW) camp in Germany. Towards the end of the war they had a system whereby you

exchanged officers. The officer could be released on parole from the POW camp and lived in a group of houses administered by the British Army in Switzerland and he finished the War there. He then went back to the Army but was mostly in a staff job.

Meanwhile having married my Mother, my brother and I having arrived, he decided to extend Hazelwood again to the North and built on the ground floor, what became the servants hall and on the first floor the nurseries, and servants bedrooms on the top floor.

If you have a look at the east end of the house you will see two limestone squares, one inscribed WGP 1921 and the other says RJP 1921. They were laid officially by my brother

Left: Sir William's father - Richard Grenville Peek 1881-1921 - in March 1921 he was shot dead by the Irish from behind a hedge.
Below: Pheasant shoot at Hazelwood. 1937. Left to Right: George Stephens, Andrew Halliday, John Welch-Thornton, Roger Peek, Charles D. Wise, William Peek.

and I. I don't remember but I'm told I said 'This stone is well and truly laid'.

In the meantime my Father rejoined his regiment in Southern Ireland and in March 1921 he was shot dead by the Irish from behind a hedge. I have a book and some newspaper cuttings written at the time giving all the descriptions of what the newspapers, both Irish and English, made of the incident. They were collected by my Father's younger Sister with whom he was very close, she put it together, I had never seen it until last summer.

Reg: You were a youngster at home at Hazelwood with your brother, what do you remember of life in those days?

Bill. We rode bicycles but it was very hard work, as you know Hazelwood is not flat!

There was, I suppose, quite a large staff, the cook and two maids in the kitchen, there was a butler and probably three housemaids, a head housemaid and two other maidens, we also had a nanny and a nursery maid, so quite a staff.

Reg. Do you remember their names? I believe Mrs Audrey Hine was here in the kitchen as a girl for a few years. When the house was for sale she came to look around and I said, "but you know the house," to which she replied, "I have never been in the front of the house, only in the kitchen."

Bill. That of course was the custom, they never came in the front of the house, the housemaids did, the butler did, but kitchen staff, no.

Below: Hazelwood House circa 1850 "Father ...had inherited Hazelwood before the First World War in 1910 ..."

Above: Richard Peek, 1782-1867 a great, great, great uncle and benefactor in building the Chapel and School in Loddiswell

Reg. Were you allowed in the kitchen?

Bill. I don't honestly remember, no, we wandered around.

Reg. Probably raiding the pantry!

Bill. Yes, maybe, but we hadn't become alcoholics then!

Reg. What staff was employed outside? You had large gardens then.

Bill. The garden above the house was Richard Peek's kitchen garden and it remained partly kitchen garden, partly shrubs but it used to grow early strawberries. Now you would never know it was ever a garden, it has become overgrown. In front of the house was a very steep formal garden with steps, which went down to the field. My Mother had part of it fenced off and made a tennis court, a spring garden for shrubs and a heather garden. It included three ponds that were fed by a spring from above the house into the top pond, then through a pipe into the second and third, and then the water found it's way down to the river.

Reg. What relation was Richard Peek?

Bill. Richard was a Great-great-great Uncle; you

see Hazelwood, as a Peek residence, stopped with him, and there was only a caretaker for 30 years because the family were either in London or they were merchants in Stonehouse, Plymouth.

Reg. When your Mother travelled was it by horse and coach?

Bill. No. The only horses we ever had at Hazelwood were riding horses, she had two hunters and we had ponies and subsequently cobs. The family I think, were slightly ahead of their time in transport, my uncle Wilfred, my Father's elder brother, had an Hispano Suiza, not only did he have a Hispano Suiza but he had an Italian chauffeur. It was an enormous Italian motor car, open car of course, with a canvas hood, I don't know what form of transport my Father had but we had a Fiat originally, again an open car, but because of the circumstances my Mother was left a widow and my brother and I were fatherless.

Luckily my Father had made an absolutely super will about a fortnight before he died, he had no premonition that he was going to get killed, that was instantaneous, but because he was going to what was regarded as a troubled area he set up a trust which eventually expired about four months ago in 1999. That had a sum of money, Hazelwood House and the property there were all incorporated into this trust, so that it had income from the farms, and two of my Father's uncles were the original trustees. It remained on course until just before the Second World War when a relative of the family from East Devon was brought in and the administration of the property was not my Mother's responsibility.

Reg. Let's go back to how your Mother travelled?

Bill. There were always two cars, one car always belonged to the Trustees and was maintained by them and my Mother had her own car and a chauffeur. There was a connection with my Mother's family; her chauffeur's Father had been my maternal Grandfather's head gamekeeper in Hampshire.

Ted Dean came after the First War, he had served in the Veterinary Corps and he then came to Hazelwood as chauffeur, he lived in the tiny cottage at the end of the stables. He was basically a horseman and when he was in the Veterinary Corps, I think he was an assistant to the qualified veterinary surgeons, he would be sent out to pick up injured horses. He was a horseman but at some stage he learned to drive.

Reg. Your tuition, was that at home?

Bill. I was always told I was unmanageable and so at the age of seven we were sent away to a boarding school at Winchester, not just next door. I am not quite sure how long I was there but then my brother and I were sent to a preparatory school at Reigate. It appeared to be the custom in those days that you sent your children as far away from home as possible, it was the accepted rule and we didn't argue. It was a very good school, the headmaster owned it. Roger was younger than me but we did everything together, when we came home for the holidays it meant travelling by train.

When my brother and I went to Eton we went to Gara Bridge, changed on to the main line at Brent to Reading. There was a wonderful main line London bound train called the Reading Slip and as the train approached the western end of Reading Station it slowed down and the Guard in the last coach, which was the Reading Slip, had an enormous level in the front of the coach, and at the appropriate moment he pulled the lever and hopefully we rode into the station. There was always a little tank engine in case we didn't make it.

I don't particularly remember when I went to Winchester or how I travelled, my Mother's family lived fairly close to Winchester so I expect we spent the night there and then she took me on from there. When I went to the preparatory school at Reigate we always spent the night with an Aunt at Reading, my Father's older sister. I remember the day before we went back to school we were taken to London to the dentist, he was an excellent dentist, I have still got ninety per cent of my teeth now. My Uncle's chauffeur would take us first to the preparatory school and then to Eton.

Reg. When you completed your tuition at Eton we were approaching the outbreak of war!

Bill. Yes, it was 1938 when I left Eton, I was then

Above: Sir William's Mother, the Hon. Mrs Joan Peek. 1892-1976

sent for three months to live with a family in France to learn French, that was the custom then, you were sent to learn a language, what use you were going to make of it, who knew? I was always destined to join the Army as a career.

Reg. You say you were destined to join the Army, was this because your Father was in the Army and you didn't have the opportunity to think about alternatives?

Bill. It was because my Father had been in the 9th Lancers and it was a family tradition that on the whole you followed your Father in his career. Equally I didn't go straight to Sandhurst, the military college, because the Uncle's had rightly decided I had a reasonable size property here at Hazelwood. We had bought Wigford and Coombe from the Woolston Estate and subsequently two farms down by Gara Bridge and eventually Aveton, which they said I ought to look after, that was of course, before anybody

anticipated there would be a Second World War. The idea was I should be equipped for both, so I went up to Oxford and was going to study agriculture; I never got as far as studying agriculture because one did a general course in the first year. Then, of course, the war came and I joined the army and I didn't come back here until 1950. It was anticipated that I should have some form of agricultural education to equip me to look after the property, as it then was nearly a thousand acres here at Hazelwood.

Reg. Of course, Roger had no choice of career because the war came!

Bill. Exactly, he was still at school, in fact both sides of the family had a military background, my Mother's Father had been a Brigadier General and her younger brother was also a soldier. Roger, in fact, joined that family's regiment, the Royal Dragoons, which at that time were in Palestine. They still had horses but by the time my brother joined them they drove armoured cars; there was a military background to both sides of the family.

Reg. Your Mother was part of the family that lived at Castle Drogo?

Bill. No, no, no that was Drewe, not a close connection with the family, Julius Drewe married a Peek, he bought a piece of land in mid Devon and then commissioned Lutyens to build him a medieval castle, a most spectacular sight, Maypole margarine paid for it, that was his business. His eldest son was killed in the first war, and his second son's eldest son, who was the same age as me, went with us to Prep School and to Eton.

Reg. Your Mother's maiden name was ....?

Bill. Slater-Booth. Her family lived near Basingstoke. Both sides of the family had political interests, because my Mother's Grandfather had been a politician and was President of the Board of Trade in the middle of the 19th century, his name started as Sclater-Booth but became Basing when he was made the first Lord Basing

Reg. So we have now moved on to the beginning of the War. Did you go to Sandhurst?

Bill. Not directly. Officer training had three different bases, you still had Sandhurst and there was still a very few of the original officer cadets who were there at the beginning of the war, otherwise you had to join the Army as a private soldier. In fact I went to the barracks at Warminster, near Salisbury Plain. My regiment, the 9th Lancers were tanks and therefore I was sent to a training regiment that had tanks just on the edge of Salisbury Plain. We had a great time there, particularly because there were six of us who were all destined to go to Sandhurst so we were put into one group together. We didn't have any special training but it was known that we were not going to become drivers of tanks but we would go to Sandhurst from where we would get a commission and then go preferably to a regiment of our choice, or to a regiment that needed officers.

Reg. You talk about that wonderful opportunity of driving around Salisbury Plain with tanks. Our son, John was on a farm, North Farm, Warminster for a period of time with the Elliotts there and they had a lowland farm and 2,000 acres of Salisbury Plain. From time to time these tanks would go across a field of wheat as well as on the Plain. He has vivid memories of going to measure up the damage for the farmer to get compensation.

Bill. Yes. We generally went on the tracks but if we went across on manoeuvres or other exercises on the Plain and damaged crops there was, at the back of the column, the gentleman representing the Army whose job it was to assess the damage for compensation.

Reg. So one way or another you avoided square bashing!

Bill. No, no, to begin with driving tanks you might say was the cream on the cake, oh no, you learnt to march and not only that but because of Dunkirk you learnt to dig First World War style trenches. We surrounded Warminster barracks so that we could have defended it against the Germans. I think it was for about ten days all trainees, staff and officers had to dig trenches. We did our training around Hampshire and then in October 1940 the First British Armoured Division left in one convoy from Glasgow. The First Armoured Division, that is to say three regiments of tanks, one regiment of light

infantry, one regiment of field artillery and various ancillary people, but we were all in one convoy. We had no problems but when we were somewhere off Brest there was a panic because one of the German long-range aircraft had been seen circling overhead. They were afraid the U Boats would know our position, but all was well and we landed at Freetown, West Africa to pick up fuel so some of us had a spell on shore. We then went on to Capetown and went ashore.

I hadn't been ashore for more than a quarter of an hour when two of my soldiers dashed up to me and said, " We've just seen your brother Sir, we have sent Smith and Jones to go and collect him, stay here." The result was that I had a couple of days with Roger, we hired a car and we toured around the Cape area. I have climbed Table Mountain, it ruined my shoes, but I can say I have walked up Table Mountain.

The convey then moved on to Suez and in fact Roger got a job taking supplies to Addis Ababa. Because he wasn't in part of a regiment, just an officer, he could get these jobs. The sad thing was that it was the last time I actually saw him when we were in Cape Town, because later on he was killed in the desert when we were retreating the first time back to El Alamein from Rommel. The border between Saudi Arabia and Egypt had an enormous barbed wire fence put up by the Italians and sometime about then the Germans had captured a lot of our transport. I only heard afterwards from his Troop Sergeant who survived and wrote to my Mother and told her what had happened. They saw what appeared to be a British lorry coming out of the dust from the west behind them and it wasn't until it stopped within a very short distance, it turned around and it had a German 15 mm anti-tank gun attached to it. It just went bang, bang, bang and shot three armoured cars and killed my brother. The desperate thing for my Mother was it was about a year before she knew if he was a prisoner or whether he was alive or dead.

Reg. That was a very difficult and traumatic time for you all.

Bill. Yes it was. We went back to Cairo, I didn't in fact take part in the battle of El Alamein because I was in hospital, not wounded but sick and rejoined round about Benghazi and then went on up to Tunis. We were left in North Africa near Algiers for nine months because the French, even in those days, were dead scared of the Arabs and they insisted on having the British Armoured Division in North Africa so that the Arabs didn't rise and throw them out, which all proved too true.

We then went across, we missed the Sicilian thing and went straight to Naples. We then drove across to Bari on the other side of Italy and then went up, in fact, fought our way up the east coast. We came to river after river because that coast has rivers running east west all the way up. We got to the next river and then we sat down for a bit and sorted things out. Then finally all the way up and we finished at Ferrara in the Po Valley. It was the most extraordinary sensation because we were fighting our way up; the war was, so to speak, perfectly normal at that time, and then night came and we both, Jones and myself, stopped. Then we heard the most enormous gunfire, but the eerie thing was no shells came our way. It wasn't until next day that we realised what the Germans had done, it was to put shells in the muzzles of their guns and burst them so that, as we advanced, they couldn't be used against them. They then boated or swam or whatnot across the Po, it wasn't very deep at that time, they went across and that was the last we saw of the Germans.

Reg. So by going up the east side you missed Monte Cassino and Anzio!

Bill. Yes. The battle of Monte Cassino was almost over before we started going up the east side and of course they had to get to Rome and past Rome before Anzio took place. We had nothing to do with either of that. We had a separate army, one went up the west coast, largely American, the army that went up the east coast was almost entirely British, although we always had Indian Divisions and very good they were too. They were British led and British equipped. The middle of the country and towards the west coast was a mixture of American and British. We were mopping up, depending how fast they went.

Italy collapsed before Germany, three or four months at least, because some of the regiments, or at least individual officers went to join Regiments in England to take part in the invasion of Normandy. We knew nothing of the invasion, we didn't know what was happening, we merely sat down, we had a few nice horses to ride, our war was over. We were an army of occupation and the Italians were not difficult, they did what they were told. The only problem was that some of the soldiers began to get friendly with the Italian ladies and automatically, if one was seen to be getting too friendly with an Italian lady, you were sent on compulsory leave to England, no argument, some said, "I have forgotten what a white woman looks like!" Only one officer in my regiment married an Italian.

Before I came out of the Army in 1951 I had a really nice job as Adjutant to the Royal Armoured Corps Gunnery School and therefore when I was deciding whether the lady now sitting beside me, would make a suitable wife, I used to spend every weekend driving like a maniac from Dorchester down to Cornwall and back again. Bovington had been a school for tanks since the First World War where cadets learned to drive tanks, we also had the wireless school there, and just at the back at Lulworth Cove you had another barracks, which was the gunnery school. The reason for that was you could fire into the steep escarpment before you got to the sea and if you missed that it went over the top and went an awful long way out to sea. One was firing almost exclusively solid ammunition; it was very pleasant there.

Reg. At that time you first came into contact with Lucy!

Bill. Yes, but her Mother and my Mother had known each other before the First World War and also I had been at school at Eton with her brother and with her cousins from the Scilly Isles, Tresco. You might say we knew the family well, but this lady, no, she had never seen me, she was only a little girl but because she was so much younger than her brother I didn't know she existed.

Lucy's Mother, living in Cornwall, used to get up boys cricket matches in the summer holidays, Devon v Cornwall with my Mother getting up the Devon team, so there had been a family connection for many years. Our two Mothers thought it would be a good idea and saw to it that there were introductions!

Reg. Lucy, what do you remember of this first meeting with Bill?

Lucy. Well, my Mother used to arrange parties for Hunt Balls in Cornwall, my Father died in 1937, two of my brothers by that time were both killed and my Mother had to deal with my sister and me. Mummy was always keen to get up parties for the Hunt Balls and it was always asked, who are we going to ask to stay for the Hunt Ball? Several times she had written to Bill's Mum to say 'Where was Bill, and could he come?' and of course he was always in Italy until he came home and then he actually came.

That year my sister's boyfriend was a brother officer of Bill's by chance, that is of course how we met and it went on from there.

Reg. You said your two brothers were killed, was this in the Second War?

Lucy. Yes, my elder brother, Richard Dorrien-Smith, was born in 1916. He joined the Buffs in 1936 and served for a while in India and then was moved back to the Middle East. He joined the 10th Battalion of Buffs and was sent to defend the coastline at Slapton in 1942-43. Richard was a Captain then and soon became bored with the inactivity so volunteered to join the Parachute Regiment. My brother was dropped at Arnhem in October 1944 and sadly was killed. Algi, my younger brother was born in 1919. He was commissioned Lieutenant Algelnon Dorrien-Smith, from Sandhurst in 1939 and joined the Duke of Cornwall's Light Infantry. He was in action through Dunkirk and then he also joined the Parachute Regiment. He was killed in a training accident in April 1942 when a pin from a hand grenade became detached and it exploded. I had twelve Dorrien-Smith cousins and, of all my cousins, nine of them lost their lives in the war.

Reg. You were in Cornwall on your estate.

Lucy. My Father fought in the Boer War and later became a Major in the King's Shropshire Light Infantry. He was invalided out of the army after the First World War and he than became a land agent; in those days you just apparently became a land agent. My elder brother and elder sister were born in Hertfordshire, Essex, my sister and I were born in Shropshire. My Father was then land agent for Sir John Carew Pole at Anthony for three years, 1928 to 1930. I suppose he then got fed up with being a land agent and decided to become a market gardener. He bought a house on the Carrick Roads between Mylor Creek and Restronguet Creek, not far from Falmouth, and grew daffodils and anemones, violets, polyanthus, cauliflowers. I can't remember how much land there was there, I suppose we possibility had five to ten acres of daffs, it wasn't big, various people worked for us picking the flowers in season. I remember bunching violets was the coldest thing on earth; it always seemed to be arctic.

Reg. You kept ponies?

Lucy. Yes, I don't remember when I was first put on a pony, probably when I was about four, learning to trot, somebody running with me saying, 'come on, up, down, up, down'. It was a little Dartmoor pony and you had a soft saddle, I think she came from Dartmoor when we were at Anthony.

Reg. You have been involved with the Children's Pony Club?

Lucy. Yes, for a long time. I was a member in Cornwall until the war, it folded during the war and my sister and I were invited to a meeting for those interested in restarting the Pony Club. It was restarted, and then, out of the blue, I was asked if I would like to instruct a course with someone else from the Club. I said, "Yes, but don't expect me to instruct," and the outcome was I had a wonderful fortnight at Porlock Riding School in 1947. Then I helped with the Four Burrows Pony Club. When I was married and came up here it was discovered that I had been helping with the Four Burrows Pony Club and I was asked to help with the Dartmoor Pony Club and so it went on from there.

Reg. You have hunted with the Dartmoor Hunt?

Lucy. Yes, almost entirely, having learnt my hunting with the Four Burrows over banks and stonewalls, that was on ponies mostly, and then for 25 years I ran the Dartmoor Pony Club, which I gave up two years ago.

Reg. **You still ride regularly with the Hunt.**

Lucy. Yes, while my horse has four legs.

Bill. And while my husband has two legs, this is my problem at the moment.

Lucy. Yes, now I have to do my own mucking out.

Reg. **I believe you used to rear pheasants?**

Bill. Yes, for about three years only, which was pre-war, because my Uncle, Harry Benyon was a very fine shot indeed and a very keen shot. He had an enormous shoot in Berkshire and his keeper taught us both to shoot and then the Trustees decided that the time had come to have what was, in those days termed a woodman keeper, who part of his time was rearing pheasants and part of his time trimming out the banks and keeping the place tidy. His name was Reed; I think he was only here for a short time. The interesting thing was that at Curtisknowle, the other side of the valley, Col. Walsh-Thornton reared a lot of pheasants; he was very keen on shooting. The great thing was their pheasant used to fly over to our side of the valley and equally ours flew over there, so we often exchanged pheasants. He kept a real gamekeeper, as opposed to just a woodman keeper.

Reg. I just mention this because my first experience of pheasant shooting was as a beater, I couldn't have been more than nine or ten years old when I was invited to come along. We stood by a copse for about three hours during the morning to ensure that any pheasants that came out rose up. Then at lunch time we went to the barn and for the first time in my life I was confronted with a pint of beer and a pasty about 18 inches long. In the afternoon I was then invited to go beating, we just went through the woods and knocked the daylights out of everything.

Bill. That's how it was in those days.

Below: Lucy Peek 'I ride with the Dartmoor hunt but I learnt my hunting with the Four Burrows Pony Club over banks and stone walls.'

Walter Kernick

Reg. I have come to interview Walter Kernick and just looking through his book, *The Ancient Kernicks of Cornwall*, I see he has details of the Kernicks right back to 1220. I see they were Abbots of Tavistock Abbey and Hartland and there were Rectors right up through the centuries. Perhaps Walter we could begin with your ancestors a bit later than that!

Walter. The Kernick family had been miners since the 1700s and my Great-grandfather grew up among Cornish miners, in fact there is one named the Kernick mine and he had a few shares in it. Miners eventually went to different parts of the world, to America or Africa, but Great-grandfather came up here to Devon, that was much easier as he could come up on a donkey and he landed himself in Lydford and then on to Widecombe where there were mines at Vitifer, and old Golden Dagger Mine. He wasn't up here very long before he married a lady from Devon and lived for a while in Lydford, then Postbridge and eventually they settled in Widecombe where descendants have remained ever since.

Reg. I have heard you mention something about digging the Severn Tunnel.

Walter. He is the same chap, in 1880 at a time

Walter's freedom of expression and indifference to the bonds of conformity bring a breath of fresh air to his life's story. Even in retirement his unbridled opinions give us food for thought. His life in the Royal Air Force has been fulfilling in his ability to do the job he enjoyed. He was born in the village and returned in retirement.

when the Severn Tunnel was going to be made, a major project; it was an awful lot of trouble, in fact it was a hell of an affair. He went up there with a lot of other fellows and took part, what he was doing I have no idea, whether he was digging with a pick and shovel. He was a mine manager at one time; he was up there for a few years and then came back again.

Reg. **Did he switch from mining to blacksmithing**

Walter. No, no this old boy's son, my Father's uncle, Richard Kernick, was born at Widecombe, and became the Widecombe blacksmith in the late 1800s. He had his own premises, which were there until the 1960s when it was all sold. He was the Widecombe blacksmith and my Father, when he was about 16, left home at Manaton and went to live with his Uncle at Widecombe to learn blacksmithing. Uncle had five daughters and they were all about the same age as my Father; he learnt his trade there finally passing his test. Do you see that piece up there that is one of his test pieces?

Then he left there and went to Torquay where he worked with a blacksmith; then later he found out that the blacksmith in Loddiswell, which was a place which could have been in

Left: The qualifying work as a farrier-blacksmith 1910 made by Fred Kernick, Walter's Father.

F. Kernick, Widecombe. 1910

outer Siberia as far as he knew, was in trouble, was either ill or collapsed and they needed a bloke there. I don't know how he found this out, as there weren't any telephones in those days. So he came down here and helped Blacksmith Kennard at Virginia Cottage.

Father eventually took over the business. He married my Mother and I was born at Virginia Cottage in 1916. I don't remember Virginia Cottage because we moved down to Rose Cottage, next to Pointridge soon after my birth; the old boy remained the blacksmith here for the next 50 years.

Reg. I remember in the 1930s I used to take the carthorses to the blacksmith's shop to be shod. Your Father always put us to work pumping the bellows while he shod the horses.

Walter. The old boy never had anything modern, the bellows were pushed by an old handle with a cow's horn nailed on the end. He never had any electricity; his grinding machine was out in the orchard and Johnnie Brown used to come down and wind the handle and throw water over the stone to grind the tools. If he wanted to work in the evening he had an old hurricane lantern and candles, no electricity whatsoever, everything by hand, it was an old fashioned, solid affair.

He wouldn't have anything to do with modern inventions. When I was older and came back and wanted something done to the car, I would go down but he would never help me, he wouldn't do a thing, he wouldn't have a car, he wouldn't

Optimum Result

The motion study expert
Looked in the smithy door
And viewed with disapproval
The litter on the floor.
He frowned upon the blacksmith
And timed his mighty swing
From lifting of the hammer
To loud metallic ring.
He noted how his waistcoat
Was splitting at the seam,
And many other details
Which showed a lack of scheme.

"My friend, you have no system,"
He told the mighty man;
"To maximise your output
You need an ordered plan.
We'll study all your movements
And draw up model rules
And re-design your bellows
And standardise your tools
We'll modernise your lighting
And regulate your hours
By statutory orders
And ministerial powers."

The smith leaned on his anvil
And spat upon his hands
(Thus wasting the saliva
Secreted by his glands.)
He said he took it kindly
That anyone should be
So anxious to diminish
His inefficiency.
And then, to show the expert
His quickness to respond,
With minimum of effort
He threw him in the pond.

Above: An anonymous excerpt from the Northcott Quarry magazine, the Northcott News (right).

Christmas Greetings

NORTHCOTT NEWS

The House Magazine of the Northcott Group of Companies

Xmas - 1955

even see the bloody things! That was my old man's view of the world.

Reg. **You spent all your younger years in Loddiswell?**

Walter. Yes, until I was 18, or 19 when I joined the Royal Air Force. I went to Loddiswell School and then to the one in Kingsbridge by train. A lot of the children went only to Loddiswell School and left when they were 14. Up until 1932 most children only went to the village schools, they didn't go anywhere else.

Reg. **Do you remember any of the pranks the boys played during your early days.**

Walter. Yes, the young teenagers were always up for a game, Bert Elliott could be relied upon to carry out many of the pranks.

I remember when I was in the Air Force and I came home on leave, we were all down at the New Bridge Inn, everybody was in there drinking including Tom Rundle and he had been well 'topped up'. When it was time for kicking out about eleven pm Bert and all his friends couldn't withhold Tom, they couldn't restrain him. He would go into the house of Mr and Mrs

Guest and say, "Could I use your phone please?" "But why at this time of night?" but Tom said, "Hold on, I want to ring the Parson." He got on the telephone to Mr Bliss and woke him up and went ahead to him. I asked Bert "What is all this about?"

"Oh this has happened before, if he gets full of drink on a Saturday night he wants to ring the Parson to tell him off. Apparently years ago when his boy was born the Rev. Bliss wouldn't christen him and Tom had remembered this all his life."

Reg. **After you left school, did you go straight into the RAF?**

Walter. No, I worked in Kingsbridge for a few years for Dick Blackler, that was about 1932. He had an ironmongers and a plumbing business,

Below: Walter's first job at John Blackler, Ironmonger, Fore Street, Kingsbridge 1932. "He (Dick Blackler) had an ironmongers and a plumbing business, laying water pipes across fields, he had agricultural binders for sale and he kept all the spare parts."

Above: Early days in the RAF with his Austin 7.

laying water pipes across fields, he had agricultural binders for sale and he kept all the spare parts.

The shop was opposite Lidstones, the butchers, it was once the Red Lion Hotel before I was born, it was one of the finest hotels in Kingsbridge, it was a huge building and was eventually divided into halves, as you see it now. On Fair days everything was put outside the shop, binders and other farm machinery drawn by horses. Down at the back of the shop was the tinsmith's shop, plumber shop, joiner shop, all sorts going on not only selling lamps etc but all sorts of tradesman's shops. Just a little further along, the other side of the passage was Warren's butcher's shop. At Christmas the geese, turkeys, pheasants and other game would be hung outside the shop.

In behind Warren's shop they had a big copper boiler where they boiled all sorts of meat and there was a chap called Thornton who worked for Blackler's, and as it was getting late Butcher Warren said to him we must make the fire out before we leave, "Throw some water on the fire and make it out," and Thornton thought for a minute and replied, "We've only got boiling water!" He didn't think that would put the bloody fire out.

In 1935 when I was a bit older I wanted to clear

off and I joined the Air Force. I went to London and was drilled like an army bloke, they all did in those days, you had to have some idea on how to fire a gun, like a soldier, everyone knew they had to put up with that for a few months because that was it. That went on for two or three months and then I went into technical training school in Kent. I was there for about 18 months, I specialised in aircraft engines, and then when I passed out they saw fit to let me loose on some aerodrome. I was posted to Salisbury and was there until just after the war started.

Reg. What type of planes were you working on?

Walter. The planes in those days were Hawker Audax, a biplane of metal construction, Hawker Hart, a two-seat light day bomber, both fitted with Rolls Royce Kestrel engines. During the time I was there the Hurricane and the Spitfire were invented and many others, like the Wellington bomber.

Then came the War and Service men were being posted away, some were left behind and some would go and join different units. I was still there in April 1940 when I had to join a little outfit which was numbered 416 Flight; eight aircraft which were going to Norway as there was fighting there. We flew around, before we got there, never got to Norway, thank the Lord, because those who did get to Norway were chased out in June, 1940 and the Air Force blokes flew their planes on to the aircraft carrier, Glorious, to come back to England, because the planes couldn't fly all the way without refuelling. The aircraft carrier Glorious was sunk with all on board, the navy blokes and most of the aircraft blokes were drowned. So I was one of the lucky ones, as I didn't go that way.

Reg. So you stayed in this country?

Walter. Of all the places to land instead of going to Norway, I ended up in Ireland; we were over there with our few planes mucking about for nearly two years on airfields near Belfast. I used to come back to England to Rolls Royce and go to Bristol Aircraft Company, and then I got mixed up with the Americans and American aircraft. One day all that ended and I was posted to Africa, where the North African War was being fought on the Tunis, Algiers side of the Mediterranean. The outfit I was with was a night fighter squadron. I couldn't fly out with my friends, engineers, electrician and the like; we had to go by boat.

We got on a minelayer to Gibraltar; the sea was so rough it damaged the Asdic receiver so we couldn't trace the submarine that was thought to be after us. We didn't know at the time that it was following us, so t'wasn't that great! It was rough in the Bay of Biscay, terrible; I'd never been there before. We went into Gibraltar to get the Asdic fixed as there were U-boats all the way around. I and some other blokes went on to a little American Coast Guard Cutter and sailed from there along the coast of North Africa for the next day or two until we came to where we were heading which was not far from Algiers.

The night we left Gibraltar we hadn't gone far when we came across a troop ship on fire the flames were pouring out. It had been torpedoed, and we found it was the Strathallen, most people on board had been saved and taken into North Africa to the port of Oran, which the British had shelled, killing 1000 French people the year before; I don't know what sort of welcome they received! The funny thing is that 50 years later when I met Bill Horton he said he was on that ship.

When I was in North Africa I was with the USA Air Force, I was lent to them for a while and then I went to Italy where I was running a completely different affair, also with the Americans, it was an American Base, I was the 'boss' of the RAF attached there. I was responsible for all the RAF aeroplanes and the South Africa Air Force. There were various things that happened there, some things blew up and big bangs and people were killed.

Eventually a RAF Transport Squadron, with Dakota aircraft, was used for everything in military transport during the war. This RAF Squadron was on this American field and was told to get out and help Admiral Mountbatten get the Japs out of Burma. I unfortunately had to join that outfit so I flew out to Burma with them and remained in Burma until the end of the war, and after the war ended. To talk about my experiences would take a month to tell you, but this is an outline of my wartime service. I was very lucky, I found myself being switched all about the place. Most of the big bangs that went off I missed them. I walked through a hanger when a stream of bullets have been coming through, somebody had been letting off a machine gun, it was sheer luck that I escaped them, I

Below: Walter and Frieda "she was a fine, strong long distance swimmer, a fine woman" with their son, Fred.

was very lucky.

Reg. **Did Bill Horton follow you out to Burma?**

Walter. Yes, he did, when we were talking recently he said, "I went across to Italy in 1943, I was there a year and then sent out to Burma until the end of the war." He came back to England. I wanted to go to Australia, I never got there, but that's another story. My parents knew I was still alive but I didn't want to return to England, I wanted to go to Australia. Bill Horton came back, I think he was a Captain in the Army and then he joined those who were running Germany. After the war there was a Control Commission of ex- Army Officers who were commissioned to control the UK Section in Germany, it was like a Military Government and he was one of them. After the war I came back to Loddiswell, I was here mucking about for some months and I thought I'm never going to get anywhere here. They used to write to me asking me to come back so eventually I went back to the Air Force of Occupation stationed in Germany.

I was there for three or four years and Bill Horton was in the same Section of Germany. During that period I met my wife and got married in Hamburg. Then my wife said to me, "Lets go back to England because that's where your parents are." I said, "I'm not going to live there, I'm going to America." She said, "OK, I'll come to America with you." We came back to Loddiswell and stayed here a few months.

It was very difficult for me to get to America, all the Americans after the War wanted to get back so there was no room for little me to get there! It was too much trouble, so eventually a chance came up, 'Go to South Africa'. I thought this is the job; I got a job there so off we went to South Africa, accepted for immigration. We were wanted there and could have stayed there for ever, that was the intention.

I went into their Air Force; if I served a number of years in their Air Force I would not be charged any fare to get there. I took the opportunity; many English blokes were taken on. To go there they had to do three years of whatever they were doing in the Air Force, and then they were free to get a job and remain

there because they had been accepted as immigrants, so that was a nice way to get there.

Reg. **Did you find any conflict between the whites and coloured peoples?**

Walter. Well there was always conflict in the Colonial Countries. The Boer War was nothing to do with colour, that was between the white people in South Africa, they were of British stock on the one hand and the Dutch. The country was managed by two lots of people, on the one side the people we call Boers, which was the Dutch word for farmer, and, on the other side, the British who got into business, especially when the diamonds and gold were found. They had a different view of life altogether; all the Boers wanted to do was to get out of the way of the British. They wanted to get out into the bundo, make themselves a farm and live there but the British would keep chasing them and eventually it came to the Boer War.

Reg. **Should we mention apartheid?**

Walter. Apartheid, that was the way things had been for a long time. In 1948 when Malan took charge, he was very much a Dutch Afrikaner bloke, and these Dutch-speaking people ran the Government, they were the main people. Dr. Malan was a minister under the British. You must remember that these old boys were very old fashioned; they wore black clothes and bowler hats. They were very strict, very much for the Church and the correct way of life, but they were a separate people, wouldn't dream of inter-marrying with black natives. It was impossible, a different view altogether of life and that's the way it was and most people grew up with these ideas, you see. I had four black chaps in the job I was doing there, they used to come in everyday and they were labourers, well, no black blokes were any other. They would give me a hand to pull and lift an engine, they were pullers and pushers, they were good chaps, they didn't get much money but we got on all right. I didn't kick them about, or anything like that. They would never have become technical blokes, it was a way of life, natives were natives then.

Reg. **Do you think it was because they didn't have the opportunity, because now the blacks**

42

Above: At work on a jet engine in the RAF 1957 "I was a Flight Sergeant, ... a chief technician in aircraft engineering, so my life was as it was before; dealing in the technicalities of aircraft, flying in them at times and sorting them out."

are taking a much more positive role?

Walter. It's a long, long story really, I'm not interested in politics at all, all I went to South Africa for was to live in the sun and do a job working and dealing with aircraft and that was the job I was given. How their Government was running their country was their business, that wasn't my worry. I had a job, somewhere to live, a good job mixed up with aircraft, I was made.

Reg. So when did politics take hold of you. You write regularly to the Western Morning News?

Walter. I'm not interested in politics at all; I'm interested in the general moral tone of the country. The country we're living in now is in a state of collapse. I write to say so and if the Editor doesn't like it he needn't print it.

Reg. He usually puts it in, doesn't he?

Walter. I've got all the examples here, and I can show you the bits he's left out! He's got to know me by this time, the last couple of letters I've written he hasn't printed at all. I can't blame him because it was some pretty rough stuff, it might upset people to read it, so I don't blame him.

Reg. You were in South Africa and then you came back to England?

Walter. Let me think now, Oh yes, we came back mainly because my wife, Frieda, had fallen and injured her back, she was in a plaster cast and all that sort of thing; it was a shame because she was a fine, strong long distance swimmer, a fine woman she's been, fell downstairs and mucked her back up. Eventually she said, "Lets go back" she loved England, she loved Loddiswell, she said "I love that little place, let's go back, I'm not well, let's go back it will be better." That was in 1952. We came back and stayed a year, and then, the same old thing, off to the Air Force again. I had to have examinations and bloody tests and interviews. They eventually told me I could go back in the Air Force with the same sort of rank as I had before, providing I could pass the necessary exams; and I did, so I was taken back because I hadn't left the Air Force for long, there wasn't a gap of more than four years so I could go back to where I left off. I went to Bedford in 1953 where Frieda joined me. Then off to Germany until 1961 and back to St Mawgan until 1963 when I retired.

Reg. **What rank were you then?**

Walter. I was a Flight Sergeant, which, in this particular case, was a chief technician in aircraft engineering, so my life was as it was before; dealing in the technicalities of aircraft, flying in them at times and sorting them out, I wasn't responsible for blokes, their discipline or telling people off.

My interests were technical, if a chap did something wrong or stupid technically it was my business to sort him out; not the way he was dressed or whether he didn't salute some bloody silly officer, that was nothing to do with me. I had stayed for eleven years, mostly in Germany and by the time I'd finished I had been long enough in the Air Force to get a pension, which has been a great thing, as I had not planned my life in this direction.

Reg. **You must have seen the transition from**

"...my chief interest in life is music, mainly music for piano and strings, and the boys who wrote it."

piston engines to jets!

Walter. Of course, yes, in fact I was one of the first to go around to various aerodromes teaching the jet world. The jet engine was simple to start with but not any more, it is so complicated I can't believe it. When Whittle invented it, it was all very simple then, the first engines were put in Meteors and De Havilland Vampires. They were fairly simple, straightforward things, they were small by modern standards. The things became huge and complicated and affected one's ears with the whining of the engines.

One of my jobs was setting up the fighter engine revs. I would be out there for an hour or two, sometimes at full blast accelerating them and setting what are known as bleed valves. I would be out there all day, then take another aircraft and do that one, blasting all the people that lived within miles of the aerodrome, they were being deafened. I was careful not to place the engine towards the place where I knew a certain young lady lived! She was a nurse in the hospital; it is all part of life's rich ...!

Reg. **It is surprising you are not deaf!**

Walter. Yes I was, I was terribly ill and I had ear trouble until three years ago and it suddenly stopped, the ear specialist in Plymouth doesn't know why. They tested my ears with all the electronic equipment, both ears were damaged, they showed the graphs.

The last time I went back I said to the specialist, "My ear troubles are all over, I can hear beautifully." I couldn't hear music for nearly a year; it was a miserable life, yet it all disappeared.

Reg. **Incredible! So your leisure time is now filled with music!**

Walter. Yes, my chief interest in life is music, mainly music for piano and strings, and the boys who wrote it. All the classical composers are here, Bach, Schubert, Mozart, Haydn, Liszt, Gounod, Chopin, Beethoven, so on and so on, those were the boys.

Reg. **Where is the Rock and Roll?**

Walter. Not at all! My metier, "Modern music is the apotheosis of inanity."

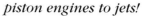

Ken Hyne

Reg. *What are your earliest recollections of Loddiswell, Ken?*

Ken. My Grandfather, Jimmy Middlewick was in Russia in the Engineers in the First World War and my Mother was born and lived at the New Bridge Inn. Jack Guest lived at the Church School House and when he bought the New Bridge Inn from his Mother, Tryphena Lakeman, the families changed houses so I was born at the School House in 1928.

I can remember my Father, Jack Hyne, had a horse and cart in the early thirties but he wouldn't take me with him, he said that's no place for kids. He kept his horse and cart down in the linhay, which is now under the Congregational Hall, and then up in Town's Lane. Before I went to school I used to play down in the Courtledge with Arthur and Charlie Brooking, we used to play chasing each other from water supply to water supply, tap-to-tap, Cowboys and Indians and that sort of stuff.

Reg. *Did you have hoops?*

Ken. Yes, old Freddie Kernick, the blacksmith, used to make them, we used to run miles with them. We played football, cricket, rounders, we used the pump for a wicket, the older boys

Ken has watched the changes evolving in the village from his early childhood and throughout his life. He grew up at School House, a central place to observe the village activities. His working life revolved around the family transport business and in later years he enjoyed playing bowls and gardening.
He and Ruth have provided the venue for the hand bell ringers for many years.

started that and we carried on. Arthur Brooking made some wooden stumps with a base so that we could stick them up on the road, they didn't fall over very easily as we only played with tennis balls, not the harder cricket balls. Annie Hine lived in a cottage at the bottom of the School Ground and her windows suffered badly, as my brother-in-law, Ted Quick, was a left-hander and always seemed to hit in that direction. Annie was George Hine's Mother, no relation to us. Our nearest relative lived in Paignton and did not have any family.

My Father worked at Holbeton for Jim Hendy's Father on their farm and when he packed up there he started in Loddiswell with a horse and cart. His first horse dropped dead and he had to borrow some money from his Aunt to buy another horse.

Reg. *You went to school at Loddiswell?*

Ken. Yes, the Headmaster was 'Boss' Bryant down at the bottom school. He had a Morris 8 and I remember 'Bumble' Brooking and 'Campie' let the tyres down on his car.

I was there for a while before Mrs Foot came and then I went to Kingsbridge School. After school I used to go down to Tunley with Herbert and Derek Harvey and when I was older, to Sid Brooking's at Greystones, in Town's Lane with Francis Hine and Malcolm Hannah.

I was 14 when I left school and helped my Father, as everything had to be loaded by hand. Tarmac and chippings from the bin at Torr Quarry had to be transported to Dartmouth and out to Bolt Head. They blasted out the stone and loaded by hand into trucks, each taking about a ton. They were on a track pulled up by a winch and tipped into the crusher. The rubbish for ballast came out one side and the blue stone, which is blue elvan, through the crusher on the other side.

Reg. When did they use lorries for transporting the stone from the face to the crusher?

Ken. Oh, it was way after the war; I went away from there and worked up at Berry Head for a few years travelling up daily. I worked for the

Above: Ken with his brothers and sisters, Ian, Tony, Maureen and Julie outside School House 1944 "I was 14 when I left school and helped my Father."

Below: . One of the earlier Hyne's lorries. "I was in the Services for nearly two years, should have been three years, but I was lucky, I came out before. There wasn't much to do back home, but then I went in with Father driving my own lorry."

Ministry of Works, Transport. (MOWT). during the war building tank stands in the woods at Lupton Park. I used to go up with Scoble's lorry because I wasn't old enough to drive. The tank stands were under the trees to provide cover preparing for D Day. That was when they built the road going down into Berry Head quarry; there wasn't a road there before, they used to go down over the cliff and send the stone away by ship. A lot of troops and equipment went away from Brixham and Dartmouth.

In July 1946 I had to do National Service. I was drafted up to Carlisle, and then across to Ballynahinch in Ireland. That was just for training, then when I passed out and moved on from there I was in the artillery on Bofors. The army had the single 40 millimetre guns; only the navy had the twins. They were anti-aircraft but they were also used against tanks.

Reg. *Did you wear earmuffs?*

Ken. No! and now I can't hear so well, they didn't think about that in those days. Sometimes we had a bit of cotton wool to stick in our ears. I was in the Services for nearly two years, should have been three years, but I was lucky, I came out before. There wasn't much to do back home, but then I went in with Father driving my own lorry. They were still kept in garages under the Chapel Hall; we used to have two of them. Father used to put a car in there to start with, but when we had another lorry we got rid of the car to make room. It was quite handy there because, if you had a bad starter you could let the brake off and shove your shoulder against the car and start 'en by running 'en down the hill towards Loddiswell Bridge.

The garages in the Courtledge were built much later, in the sixties.

Reg. *Then, of course, lorries became larger and larger. Did you drive articulated lorries or stay with tippers?*

Ken. I stuck with the four-wheelers, the others went up the road, I wanted to stay local, hauling stone, concrete blocks and sand until I retired in 1991, that was just after the firm moved up to Robin's Park.

After we were married we lived in Virginia Cottage for a couple of years, that's where Frank Carpenter lives now. Richard was twelve months old when we moved up here to Ashwood Park. Let's see, what is Richard now? Forty-one years old, so we have lived here for about 40 years. It was 1959 when we moved in here and Roger Taylor moved out to go over to number 30 where my brother, 'Knocker', is now. When we moved in here they were building Miss Michell house, Pendarvis in Village Cross Road, I remember it was a very hot summer.

Since I've retired I have played bowls, that is until my knees went wonky. I spend a bit of time in the garden and have been interested in the hand bell ringing team, which started in the early 1970s and they've played in many village halls. So that is it!

You may wonder how my brother 'Knocker' got his nickname. his actual name is Ian Hyne, but his pals called him Enoch and then this changed to 'Knocker'.

Below: Ruth, Ken's wife, lace making.

Nellie Baker

Reg. You have lived in Loddiswell most of your life, Nellie.

Nellie. I was born in Loddiswell, here at Vine House, as was my older sister Flora and my brother John (Bill). When we were at Loddiswell School my sister, brother and I would visit my Auntie Nell, (her maiden name was Ellen Kennard) and Uncle George Hingston who lived at Greystones Farm. We used to go down over the field hedge into the orchard instead of down the road, to see Uncle's brother, Tom Hingston, filling up bags of coal to sell around the village. The coal used to come by train to Loddiswell station and Tom fetched it from there with Uncle's horse and cart. Everyone then used coal, as there was no electricity in Loddiswell at that time. Sometimes we saw them shearing sheep there. Miss Stone and then Mr. Bryant taught us at Loddiswell, then we went on to Kingsbridge school and I left when I was 15 and came home to help my Father look after the cows and poultry, and do the necessary work in the fields and gardens. I also helped Mother indoors but I would like to have gone on to school like my brother and sister. Flora sadly died at Exeter University at the age of 19 and my brother John went to London University. When we left he went into the Army where he rose to the rank of Captain. He served in the 1939-45 War in France, Italy and in Malaya but I did not see him for several years as he was abroad.

How many people can recall such a distinguished line of ancestors? Nellie has been able to account for them, not only the seven blacksmith brothers born in the 1800's, some emigrating to Australia, New Zealand and the USA but all their families. Her life story includes a wonderful collection of photos and memories.

In 1947 we went to Bloxwich for my brother's wedding to Elizabeth Owen and I was one of the bridesmaids. They met when they were both working in the German Control Commission after the War. I remember we stayed with my cousins Loveday and Percy Libby; he worked as the local Planning Officer for Warwickshire for many years. We all went to Stratford-on Avon to see Ann Hathaway's Cottage and to Wolburn Abbey. My Father died in 1949 so my Mother sold the cows. My Aunt Ella Kennard, who was a retired school teacher at the Priory School at Torquay, sold 'The Cottage' in Town's Lane where she had lived and came over to live with my Mother and me at Vine House. Later that year, 1949 my Mother died.

Albert James Baker and I were married in 1955 and went to live at West Redford. Kingsbridge. Our honeymoon was in Bournemouth and then in London where we attended the Armistice Service at the Cenotaph on the Sunday. We saw the Lord Mayor's Show while we were there as it processed around the streets of London.

Above: Nellie and Bert with James and Francis.
1965

Our elder son James was born at West Redford, and when my husband semi-retired we moved back to Loddiswell where he kept some cows and poultry. I enjoyed helping with them until Francis, our younger son was born. James was very pleased to have a brother.

Below: James, Nellie and Francis. 1996

In 1979 we all went to stay in Bedford for the wedding of Patrick, my brother John's son, to Angela in London. We visited Blenheim Palace where Sir Winston Churchill was buried and on to Shuttleworth aerodrome where there is a large collection of early aeroplanes; then to a huge hanger near Bedford where the airship R 101 was built, before a visit to Cambridge University.

My husband Albert died in 1986 and Francis still lives with me at Vine House. He is an electronics engineer for a local firm in Totnes while James, who lives in Gloucester, is a manager of a shop belonging to Threshers, part of the First Thirst Group.

We are able to trace the Horton side of the family back to 1600 at Cornwood. My Great-grandfather Trobridge Horton and Great Uncle John Horton left their father at Dinnaton Farm, now a Country Club near Ivybridge, to move to East Allington. Great Uncle John farmed Burleigh Farm and my Great-grandmother Mary had the shop. A ledger from the shop is on loan to the Cookworthy Museum and is displayed in the kitchen area showing a list of groceries for Mrs Fortescue at Fallapit. Mary's daughter Eliza took on the shop after her.

My Grandfather, John, married Sarah Codd of Lower Pool, East Allington and had the Fortescue Arms, a wheelwrights' business and Bunkers Farm, which, in recent years has had a number of houses built on its ground. All the tools from the wheelwright's shop are also on loan to the Museum.

He also bought this place, Vine House, here in Loddiswell in 1872 and also the Malt House which he converted into No 1,2,3 and 4 Vine Terrace. Vine Cottage is in between Vine Terrace and our house, it is where the Malt Manager lived.

When both my Grandparents had died my Father and Uncle John sold up their businesses at East Allington and came to live at Loddiswell Grandfather had bought two thatched cottages further up Town's Lane, South View, where my Father Trobridge Horton had lived before he married my Mother Clara Poloina Kennard. As well as farming the small holding my Father

collected the Rates from everyone in the village. That was before we paid a Community Charge to South Hams District Council.

I was rather annoyed in later years when the tenants of South View Cottages moved to new houses in Ashwood Close and the Kingsbridge Rural District Council condemned the cottages and knocked them down before the thatcher, whom Mother had engaged could repair the thatch.

At the time the Council paid my Mother £50 for the both of them. My cousin Percy said that if the cottages had been in Warwickshire they would not have been knocked down, there would have been a Preservation Order on them. The Kennard side of the family in Loddiswell dates back to 1664 on the Church Registers. Great-grandfather John Kennard married

Above: Great-grandfather John Kennard and his wife Elizabeth with their seven sons Left to Right they are: Frederick (Loddiswell), William (Nellie's Grandfather), Robert (USA.1870), James (New Zealand 1870), Richard (New Zealand), Noah (Kingsbridge), George (Woodleigh).

Elizabeth Harvey and they had seven sons.

Their first son Frederick married Elizabeth Bowden and carried on the blacksmith business after his father retired. They had one son and three daughters and lived at Virginia Cottage where the blacksmith shop was adjoining. The Kennards were in charge at that time of the Village Pound, which was situated at the back of the blacksmith shop.

Any stray animals were put there until the owners collected them later and paid a fine.

Frederick and Elizabeth's son John went to a friend's funeral and had pneumonia and died, he was 25 years old. This was, of course, before the days of penicillin. His widow took their two daughters, Margery and Freda to London where Margery eventually married a Dr. John Marks.

The second son, William Kennard, was my Grandfather who married Rosina when working in Torquay. They had one son, Frederick who married Charlotte and they had three daughters, Ellen married George Hingston and my Mother Clara Poloina, of course married Trobridge Horton.

The third son Robert married Leah Goodman and they went to America in 1870. Their Great-grandson Larry and his wife Marlyn Welsh stayed in Kingsbridge and came to visit us four years ago. Paul, their son had looked up the family history and found that his Great- great-grandfather was John Kennard of Loddiswell so they wanted to see where he lived.

The fourth son James married Amelia and emigrated to Dunedin in New Zealand in 1863. They called their house 'Loddiswell' to remind them of their roots and the house is still there. They have two sons Frederick and Harry and two daughters.

Harry was a tutor at a Technical Institute in Dunedin, he married Christine and they have two sons, Walter and Barry and one daughter Sunnette. She came to England in 1998, and after travelling all over Europe she went to Scotland where her Mother's family lived, they stayed for a few days in London before she came to Loddiswell to stay with us. She went to Church on the Sunday to see where her ancestors had worshipped and to Virginia Cottage to see where her Great-grandfather was born. She has three nephews, Scott, Wade and Glen, so, with her brother Walter there are at least five Kennards carrying on her family name for a further generation.

In the Milton Gazette which covers an area near Dunedin, there was a report in 1973 about the family, "The Milton Smithy, still in Kennard hands, was started by Kennard and Sons 107 years ago and still stands on the main street of Milton."

The fifth son Richard went to New Zealand in 1869, six years after his brother James. He had sons Frederick and Alfred and three daughters. Frederick had three daughters, one, Freda is now 93 years old and still drives her car to Church and shopping in Auckland. Freda has two daughters, a grandson, a granddaughter and four great -grandchildren.

Alfred married Connie and they have two sons, Harry was a barrister and married Mary, they had a son Barry. Allan, my second cousin, never married, he was a prisoner of war in the 1939-1945 War.

After the war he stayed in London at New Zealand House for several years. When the High Commissioner went back to New Zealand on holiday Allan was in charge in his place. We saw Allan several times while he was over here. They all came down to Plymouth to stay and visited Loddiswell. After he returned to New Zealand he worked for the Government until he retired.

The sixth son Noah George Kennard was a blacksmith and farrier in Kingsbridge and his son George continued the farrier work and developed a riding school. Leslie Kennard, his son, moved to Somerset with the riding school and trained racehorses.

The seventh son George was the blacksmith at Woodleigh and has a daughter. Sadly the local name of Kennard in England has almost disappeared in our family.

There was another branch of Kennards who lived in Loddiswell who we think were descendants of our Great-grandfather's brothers. The last of the family that lived here were children of a Richard and Agnes Kennard. Their son James, who was a farm worker at Yanston, Loddiswell married Catherine, a schoolteacher in Cornwall.

They had eight children, James, Charles, Sam, Herbert, Walter, Susan and Violet. Five of the sons all served in the 1914-18 War and fortunately all returned home safely at the end of the War.

James married Laura Yelland and lived at Sunnydene, Station Road, Loddiswell.

He served in the Navy until he retired and then was a gardener for Col. Wise at Alleron. When Laura died James's sister Susan came to live with him at Sunnydene. She had retired as Post Mistress at Loddiswell. Charles went to Canada and joined the Canadian Army and he had two sons. Kenneth, the elder of the two came over and joined the Air Force in the 1939-45 War, but sadly his plane was shot down and he was killed. His younger brother worked for the Canadian T V until he retired.

Sam served in the Canadian Navy until he retired and then returned to England.

Herbert served with the Worcester Regiment and then he and his wife, Winnie went to Canada farming but came back to England a few years ago. Walter and William served in the Royal Navy before they went farming in Canada and their families are still out there.

Violet Elizabeth Kennard married Albert James Baker of Hazelwood and they emigrated to Canada and farmed in Saskatchewan from 1925–37. Their daughter Phyllis was born there and they returned to England when she was still small. They farmed Bridgecombe, near Loddiswell before moving to West Redford, Kingsbridge where Violet died. Their daughter Phyllis married Kenneth Court, an architect in Kingsbridge and they have two sons Nigel, and Michael who married Elaine, they have a son Adam.

Phyllis's younger sister Monica married John Luscombe and they farm at Overbrent, South Brent. They have two sons, John and Robert and two daughters, Susan and Jane. In 1995 Monica wanted to visit the place in Saskatchewan where her Father had farmed, so she placed an advertisement in the local press over there to see if anyone remembered Bert Baker. She received a reply so her daughter Susan accompanied her to Canada and they stayed with the Nelsons who farm the land.

At the time of Monica's first visit some of the farm implements were still in place in the yard, just as they had been left after the farm sale in 1937. The dry cold weather had preserved them in good condition. They were no longer there on Monica's second visit a few years later and the timber barn, which was leaning badly on the first visit, had been dismantled.

Below: Bert Baker's farm in Canada. 1937. In 1995 Monica wanted to visit the place in Saskatchewan At the time of Monica's first visit some of the farm implements were still in place in the yard, just as they had been left after the farm sale in 1937. The dry cold weather had preserved them in good condition. They were no longer there on Monica's second visit a few years later ...

Walter Hine

Eveline, Walter Hine's wife, passed away in April 2001. Walter, born in 1911 and now 92, is still able to live with a little help at Arundell Place.

Reg. **I've come this afternoon to No 16. Arundell Place to see Walter Hine and his wife Eveline. Walter I know is a member of a fairly large family.**

Walter. That's true, brother Bill, sister Ethel, sister Doris and then myself, sister Emily and twins Leonard and Leslie.

Reg. **Where did you live when you were youngsters?**

Walter. Well, Father was a gardener and moved around to different houses. At one time he was a gardener for the Loddiswell Church vicar when they lived over at Chantry. The vicar then provided a pony for Father to ride forward and back because he was crippled. I was actually born in Woodleigh Mill, and then we moved up to where Winnie Jeffery is now, called Sunnyside. We have also lived up at No 4 Town's Lane, then we moved down to Alleron and in 1919 we moved from Alleron to Hazelwood. Father was second gardener at Hazelwood and we went to Loddiswell School but I don't remember my school days much before that. Later when we were out at Hazelwood we walked three miles each way.

Reg. **You must have remembered the Walkes of Hazelwood?**

Walter has lived a full life, kind and generous in nature. His contribution to the village has been immeasurable, unassuming but always willing to lend a hand.

His war service years have been unknown and we are privileged that he has recorded, for posterity, his exploits over enemy territory throughout the Second World War

Walter. No, they were older, I remember the Bakers of Higher Hazelwood, Alan and Mary, we probably walked together if we met; they used to walk through the drive on the same path as we did.

Reg. **Did you go on to Kingsbridge school?**

Walter. No no, Loddiswell all the time. When the twins were old enough to go to school, Mrs Joan Peek, that's Bill's Mother, provided a donkey for me to take the twins to school. We had a field to keep him in at the bottom of the drive. We would go down and sometimes the donkey would go quite nicely but sometimes he was quite awkward, he wouldn't go outside the gate. So I would turn him around and give him a slap across the backside and send the children back home again, and I'd walk on to school. When the donkey was in a good mood he'd take the children to school and we would park him in the stables under Sunnyside, that's where the Handy Shop is now. He'd stay there until after school and then we would go home again.

I went to school until I was thirteen and then I worked out on a farm at Blackwell Parks for three months for Charlie Thomas who was managing the farm for Capt Conran who lived at

Above: Chauffeur at Dodbrooke Manor,
Kingsbridge 1930 for Major and Mrs Stapleton-
Cotton. "I stopped there for nine years as
chauffeur/gardener driving their 30 hp Daimler."

Woolston House. I didn't like it there so Father got me a job in Kingsbridge at the Knowle; I went there as a garden boy and I spent three years there.

When I was 17 Father went with me to see Bill Bevil, a Loddiswell man, who was head gardener at Dodbrook Manor, the home of Major and Mrs Stapleton-Cotton and I stopped there for nine years as chauffeur/gardener driving their 30 hp Daimler.

When I left there in June 1937 I went to work for J W Guest at the Egg Packing Station in Loddiswell. I really started at the end of May but we got married on June 12th and I worked for them until the outbreak of war. I did lorry work for Guests for different Councils, it was the Urban District Councils (UDC) then, Totnes, Kingsbridge and Plympton, we would go where we were wanted.

Then in the middle of 1939 the lorries were commandeered and I went to work for Kingsbridge Urban District Council driving a lorry collecting old iron, rags, bottles anything for salvage, for the war effort.

Between times I used to go out to Portlemouth with the lorry and load up with long poles to carry around to the cliffs. A gang of men would come around at the weekend and sink them in to prevent the aircraft from landing. We went to all the high spots from Malborough to Dartmouth where a craft could quite easily land.

*Reg. **Then fairly soon you were called up?***
Walter. I was called up in September 1940. I left my son Michael, two years old, and baby daughter Muriel, three months old, with my wife at home.

*Reg. **You went in the Army?***
Walter. Yes, that's right, went to our barracks and got put in a squad there, then switched just across the valley from Bulford Camp to Carter Barracks, which was our depot. I was put in the Royal Army Service Corp (RASC) Transport Division and did my month's training there.

Then I was offered a job as a driving instructor at Perham Down so I accepted it, and in early 1943 our RASC Driving Instructors Unit moved up to Matlock, Derbyshire the Regimental HQ. I did umpteen routes up there in the same capacity, a different route for each day of the week, except Sundays. That went on until the middle of 1943, when we were switched down next door to DeHavilland, aircraft factory. Twenty of us went down, we didn't volunteer, it was 'you, you, you and you are going down there'.

There was an old fuselage there of a Dakota C 47 and we practised with sand bags loading it up and unloading it. Eventually we formed the Dakota Air Drop, that was the first group that was formed and we trained other groups. We would fly out and drop between two cross roads. No one was allowed in the dump, it was sealed off at each end by a guard, and in that dump there was stored any amount of supplies, ammunition, medical supplies, food, first aid and stuff that they needed, and it was on duck boards. There were 16 panniers in a stack, which was one load for the aircraft, and they were 350 pounds apiece. We had to do a lot of practice first with sandbags on the panniers on the dummy runs and then we were using real stuff, they were like big laundry baskets with rope corners to carry them upside-down to the transport plane where they were fitted with a parachute. Eventually we did fly across but while we were training there was many a pound lost and won on bets as to who could drop the quickest load. You might've believe it, but it was perfectly true, there was one chap down there who could tell exactly when I dropped. Very often I would be the last, not because there was any reason for it, but because the pilot would go around and fly over the dropping zone, which was a big T and when he got over the nose of the

Below: Douglas Dakota. "There was an old fuselage there of a Dakota C 47 and we practised with sand bags loading it up and unloading it. Eventually we formed the Dakota Air Drop, that was the first group that was formed and we trained other groups."

big T he allowed us to begin dropping. As he went on it drifted back the stem of the T according to the wind. One chap would always bet on my load as the quickest time, and, as I said very often we would be the last, to go round. The quickest time was six seconds dropping 16 panniers in one load all coming down together and that was my gang. It consisted of a Corporal, Lance Corporal and two drivers. The pallets were all strapped in on roller conveyors at the bottom of the plane and if you worked with the pilot it was easy but if you didn't work with him it could make it very awkward.

We daren't move any panniers until he gave us the green light and then we'd move one stick down to the door ready to go out and everyone had to do his job right on the dot. There was a gate to change down at the bottom, there were two roller conveyors coming down and they joined into one, it was like points on the railway line. These gates had to be changed one up, one down as quick as lightning. When the green light came on we could start working but if the red light came on we had to stop. I can tell you there was no hope of seeing a red light because we were too fast; everything was out in six seconds.

Reg. You were dropping before the Normandy

Landings on June 6th. 1944.

Walter. Yes, we were dropping in this country, practising. When we went over the other side, we didn't know where it was, well, we couldn't pin point it. We used to fly across from here.

On this particular occasion we went to an airfield where they kept Stirling aircraft. We left camp at eight o'clock in the evening and we got to the airfield and we got on the aircraft at half past ten at night. The aircraft took off and I don't know where we went, we must have been up with the birds. At midnight, as we flew down over France, the sky was lit up over on the right and the pilot said the German base for their U-boats under the concrete bunkers at St Nazaire had been bombed that day and were left blazing.

We travelled on to an unknown destination and when we had the instructions from the crew the Second Lieutenant Johnnie and myself had one pannier each to drop out. In the bomb cells of the Stirling aircraft there weren't live bombs but there were bomb cell containers containing medical supplies, radios, ammunition, rations anything that was needed for the troops. The pilot released those at the same time as we released our two panniers. I said to Johnnie you drop first and I'll drop second, so we did and after we'd dropped we flew, and flew and flew and we landed at six o'clock in the morning at the airfield where the Stirling took off from.

We went back to our camp and Johnnie was in the company office, I went to try to bivouac. After a while at nine o'clock we were going up to the canteen in the marquee and Johnnie happened to see me passing and he shouted, "Do you know where we went last night, Wally?" I said, "No, I haven't got the foggiest idea." He said, "We went down to Anzio in Italy." I would never have believed it, well, I didn't realise that there was enough fuel in the aircraft to be flying all those hours, but any rate we done our job and landed safely.

Reg. That would have been when Eisenhower and Montgomery had landed at the Anzio beachhead between January and May 1944.

Walter. Yes, Monty was making his push at that particular time at Anzio.

Above: In the Royal Army Service Corp Transport Division. 1942

Later we were dropping at the Falaise gap near Caen. It took us 45 minutes to fly to Arnhem so after the invasion they commandeered the Belgian Airport at Evere and we went out there. We packed it, loaded it, went up and dropped it at Nijmegen and then at Arnhem. I was up twice one day with my gang and they wanted volunteers to do a night drop. I didn't hear about it but my gang said if we can get Wally to go we'll

Below: Walter's brother and sisters. Left to Right. Walter, William (Bill), Doris, Ethel, Len, Les and Emily. 1981

go, so we did, we had three jobs at Arnhem in 24 hours. I was due for leave before I went across, so I was one of the first to come back and I can tell you I've never had a ride so comfortable as coming back in that plane. It was loaded with used parachutes, pure silk parachutes and it was loaded up as full as it could possibly be, and the aircraft crew had to climb back over to get to the cockpit. I was up there within two foot of the roof of the plane, lying on used pure silk parachutes.

I came back and went on leave, then I went back again and was there in the camp, doing general things and then all of a sudden the Germans broke through the Zuider Zee Barrier and they flooded some of the lands. When we went there we had to drop large sacks, very stiff sacks, and they were thrown out loose, no parachutes. We went in as low as we possibly could and as slow as we possibly could and we threw these out, we had them stacked up in the doorway, and if we had half a dozen we had time to do it. Out went half a dozen; if there was a technical hitch we would have been only able to throw out four or five. Then we would stack up some more by the doorway, I think there was about 25 sacks all told for the load. When we dropped one lot we came in again and dropped again. Now this is something I shall never forget; when we finish dropping the pilot said, "Grab hold to something," and he circled around, 'course there was no door on the aircraft, it had been taken off. He circled around so we could look out the doorway on her side so we could see the people underneath. To see those people looking up to the aircraft waving, grateful for what we were taking to them I shall never forget, it brought tears to my eyes.

Reg. **That was towards the end of the war, when did you come home again?**

Walter. February 1946. I had done five and a half years. I went back to W J Guest, and worked for Devon County before they bought their own lorries, we were out on hire to them. We could go anywhere in the Plympton, Totnes or Kingsbridge area, but we were further afield most times; wherever they wanted us that was where we had to go. Gradually the council got their own lorries.

In 1957 I took over the milk lorry and collected milk around the area in churns, I started here in the village, went to North Huish, Ugborough, Modbury, Avonwick, South Brent, Harberton and then worked my way to Totnes. I was picking up churns all the time, it was two loads everyday, not quite full, but in the summer when there was plenty of milk about I did three loads. I wouldn't finish until three in the afternoon. Didn't matter what happened, I went in first thing in the morning, I was my own boss and all I had to do was to get the milk there, that was my problem. I had to get the last lot in there at half past three. That went on until 1974 when I unfortunately had an accident and hurt my back.

Reg. **Lifting around these churns, I expect?**

Walter. Yes, it was one day when it was wet; in fact it was the same day I was going on holiday. I was at a certain milk stand which was 18 inches wide, on a wall, the churns measured thirteen and a half inches wide, so it didn't give me much room to stand between them. The old farmer used to moan because I threw the empty churns in the field and he had to go in there and pick them up, that was not my problem. I was putting this churn on and it was a horrible day, wet, and I got behind it and stuck two toes in between three churns and tilted it back. It was two inches lower and I pushed the churn up, and because it was wet and slippery the churn slid away and didn't go straight up as I wanted it. I went to save the churn with the milk and I rolled on my back instead, never wasted the milk. That was in 1974, it was 20 months before I was due to retire, and that was the end of my working life.

Reg. **Where did you live when you retired?**

Walter. Ashwood Park. I went to Courtledge in 1937 and No 1 Ashwood Park in 1947, which was when the houses were just built. I lived there for 23 years until 1970, then I came down here to Arundell Place and lived here ever since.

Reg. **You have been an active member of the Over Sixties Club!**

Walter. Yes, you could say that. I was secretary for 15 years and enjoyed it.

Herbert and Sheila Harvey

*R*eg. *This afternoon I have come to Orchard View to talk to Herbert and Sheila Harvey. I know a little about Tunley as I was born here but we left when I was two and a half years old so I don't remember too much about it. Where were you born Herbert?*

Herbert. I was born at Lower Kellaton, Stokenham in 1925 and I was two and a half when they brought me to Tunley in 1928. I don't remember any thing about Kellaton although we have been back a few times. I understand my Mother used to push me in the pram down to the beach at Lannacombe.

My earliest recollections of Tunley were of attending Loddiswell School, I was four years old when I began. When my Father took me there he said, "You go on and I'll catch you up on the pony," and when we got to Loddiswell Butts the pony slipped on the main road and he fell off and injured his shoulder. He said, "I can't go any further, you better manage to go on your own." I said, "I'll try," so I had to go to school on my own. The only person I knew there was Mrs Dorothy Taylor so that was my first day at school. Father had cracked his collarbone.

Herbert gives a vivid account of traditional farming and the revolutionary change into modern mechanisation, which he experienced during his teenage years. His love of livestock quickly encouraged him into the improvement and judging of cattle and participation in local agricultural shows.

Shelia's great love of farming surfaced at an early age and her commitment has been maintained throughout her life.

Reg. *What do you remember of school?*
Herbert. I was a fairly big boy and eventually was made a prefect. I helped to look after Gordon Taylor who was in a wheel chair as he suffered from Muscular Dystrophy. As my birthday was the 23 September and the school year began on the 10 September I had to stay at Loddiswell an extra year, which I felt was wasted.

I began Sunday school at Loddiswell Congregational Church but my cousins the Perrings at Lixton went to Aveton Gifford Methodist Sunday School so I joined them there. My brother and I used to ride the pony down there on Sundays afternoons.

During those years I had to help on the farm. Father expected me to work when I came home from school and at the weekends and holidays, feeding the cattle and looking after the horses. I was not allowed to go up to the village playing football.

After Loddiswell School I went to Kingsbridge Modern Secondary School. I had so many friends in Loddiswell School that I wanted to keep with them. They didn't want to take the exam so we kept together. As time went on I thought I would like to be a Vet. but when I was

Above: Tunley Farm House "I was two and a half when they brought me to Tunley in 1928."

fourteen in September 1940 Father wanted me home on the farm. The war had started and I remember we had to take our gas masks to school.

When I left school I worked with horses, drawing mangolds and turnips to the stock; doing field cultivations. We used a tormentor for ripping arrishes after the corn harvest, rolling and harrowing ground to get it ready for sowing corn and root crops. Ken Hyne used to come down from the village most weekends; he would drive the horse and cart while I threw out the turnips to the cattle. I looked forward to

Below: Mother, Nell, providing the 'drinkings' for the boys in the harvest field. c.1933

that, two boys together; we had a bit of fun. He still remembers the names of all the horses. It is surprising how much was expected of us at the age of 14. We were expected to be grown up but now life has changed.

When I was 16 I put on my age so I could join the Home Guard. There wasn't much to do home here and I enjoyed going to it. Looking back over the years I wonder if it was really worthwhile. There were one or two whom I wouldn't trust with a gun, they might shoot me. Sometimes rifle practice was at Yanston where we fired across the valley into targets in the side of Idestone Hill field. On one occasion Sergeant McCandles was over in the slit trench by the targets and he signalled back, "What's happening to your shots, they aren't hitting the target." Wilfred Paynter shouted back, "They'm leaving here alright."

I joined voluntarily but some were compelled to join and some were not very interested. I was given a cup-discharger, which was fitted on to the rifle to fire grenades, but I never fired it, so what good I would have been I don't know!

Reg. If you had to, you would have used it.

Herbert. Yes. I probably would. I remember we had to spend a night once a week in the Old St Edmund's Rectory up near Plymouth Road; it was empty and rather derelict. There was a telephone there and if a message came through we would have to take it to the old British Legion School in Church Street where a Home Guard section was on duty. Why they couldn't have a phone there I don't know!

When they bombed Aveton Gifford I was working horses in a field near Fernhill Cross, the plane came across, I could see the pilot and the swastika on the side, it frightened the horses and they took off. I saw the bombs leave the plane but I didn't know what they had hit. I later heard they had bombed Aveton Gifford Church. On the farm we were one of the first to have a tractor, which was in 1941, I believe. Nobody knew a lot about mechanics of tractors so we had to teach ourselves. I joined the Young Farmer's Club in Kingsbridge when I was 16 and I learned a lot there about ploughing because my Father couldn't teach me anything about a three-furrow trailer plough. I was able to compete in the Club's ploughing competitions with a three furrow Lister plough. I also learned thatching there from a thatcher at Chillington. I remember thatching at Sorley I was one side of the rick and Joyce Dellar, who married William Heath, was the other side thatching. I used to carry her bundles of reed up for her and then I discovered some of mine was disappearing, she was pinching it from over the top and laying it on a bit thicker!

I did stock judging with South Devons. Seale Hayne had wanted us to judge Channel Island breeds but Mr Bert Camp Snr said, "Why can't we use our local breed?" So we judged South Devons, which were in those days dual-purpose animals. They produced quite a lot of milk with good butterfat and still produced good beef.

We were married in 1954.

*Reg. **Wait a minute, how did you meet Sheila?***

Herbert. Well, that's another story! I had a girl friend that I'd been with for years and Sheila came to work as a student over at Wizaller for Mrs Goss. She wanted to join the Young Farmer's Club and I was Chairman at the time. When I was at Kingsbridge Market one day Mrs Goss introduced me to her and we both went the same way. I had to explain to my girl friend what had happened.

When I was married my Father retired. By that time we were able to buy the Glebeland that we had previously rented. My brother, Derek, stayed with us for the next ten years until he wished to get married. A farm was purchased and he took half the stock. This created a situation which I had not been used to and money wasn't so free. We eventually paid off the overdraft and my brother had a farm of his own. It was a good idea to go our own ways especially as our families grew up.

*Reg. **Your Father was one of the first people to have a car in the area? Do you remember what make it was?***

Herbert. It was a Wolsley Hornet, he bought it from Mr Wise of Alleron who used to change his car every two years. That was pre-War about 1936 and Mr Pearse of Oke's Garage taught him to drive. I eventually learned to drive on my own; I never had to pass a test. There weren't any tests during the war and not many police around in those days.

Although petrol was rationed I could get it to go to Young Farmer's Club lectures and training sessions. I was Chairman for three years in the late forties, early fifties and although petrol was still rationed I was able to get extra coupons from Tug Wilson who was County Organiser. I was interested in public speaking and stock judging and I used to go around judging at different shows

*Reg. **In more recent years you have been very associated with Kingsbridge Show.***

Herbert. I was President in 1988 after being Vice-Chairman and then Chairman. I had been a Steward for the Show for 40 years, mainly in the cattle section. Now I'm a Life President.

During my farming life I met many of my friends at Kingsbridge market, but later the trade moved to Newton Abbot where there were more buyers so we went there to sell our stock.

*Reg. **Sheila, you were not a Loddiswellian!***

Sheila. I almost needed a passport to get here as I was born in Bristol. My parents had, what would now be termed a semi-supermarket, they had a petrol station behind it, petrol pumps and a forecourt. It was a very large building, four storeys high and when the bombing started we used to go down to the cellars underneath as soon as the sirens went. Many of the people in the street would come down into the cellar with us. Bristol was very badly bombed, the whole sky was lit up with the flames, we could see it from our windows. We were some way out of the centre of Bristol and the nearest bombing we had was the Bishop's Palace which was just about a mile away from where we lived.

My Father was an Air Raid Warden and was often on duty in the city. I was about ten years old at that time. The junior school where I went was severely bombed and we then had to take our schooling in a private house, which the school took over until the end of the war. I stayed on in the senior school until I was 16.

My parents sold the business and moved to Preston, near Paignton and then I came as a student to Mrs Goss's at Wizaller. Later my parents came to Loddiswell having bought Court House and although Father died sometime later, Mother was there for 27 years.

Reg. Why did you want to go on a farm?

Sheila. During my childhood I had gone to my Father's cousin's farm and being an only child I was put on the train at Templemead Station, Bristol and then my cousins would meet me at the other end in Cornwall to spend every summer holiday down on their farm. I suppose I had a liking for it then; it seemed to be in my blood. I always say I am a countrywoman by adoption.

My work at Mrs Goss's was dairy work; she had Jerseys but mainly Friesians. We were milking about 40 or 50 and had the help of a herdsman. It was machine milking; I only milked by hand when visiting my cousin's farm in Cornwall. I stayed there for 18 months and during that time I met Herbert at Kingsbridge Market.

We were married in 1954 and that was 49 years ago next week. I can't think it is so long ago until I see my children and ten grandchildren, the eldest is now 22 years old, then I can believe it. Fortunately Paul has taken on the farm and he has a wonderful wife who helps him and four lovely children.

I get a lot of enjoyment from the Women's Institute and the Over Sixties, which we go to in the village. I am co-ordinator for the Neighbourhood Watch, and we do quite a bit for the Congregational Church. I love gardening but my main hobby is walking the dogs, I am a dog lover. They give me a lot of pleasure and they keep me fit, as I do several miles a week.

Below: 'My interest in showing and judging cattle started early in my life. This bull was the Champion bull of all breeds at the Yealmpton Show in 1963'

John Webber

Reg. This morning I have come to Kerowell in Well Street, Loddiswell not very far from Lod's Well, the well that was renovated as a Millennium Project. I've come to talk to John Webber. John, have you always lived in Loddiswell Parish?

John. No. My Father came down here from Chumleigh in 1910 and married a Kingston girl, he was a farm worker and they moved to Pittaford, Slapton where I was born. Then he moved on to the Co-op farm of Scobbiscombe at Kingston and stayed there until 1947 when I was thirteen. The Manager there was Joe Bennett and the farm was part of the Plymouth Co-operative Society farms that supplied milk to Plymouth. I went to Kingston School as a junior and then on to Modbury. I had another year and a half to do when we moved to Loddiswell so I went to Kingsbridge Senior School. When I left school I went to work at Reads Farm for Mrs Griffin for the next 15 months poultry farming. I had helped her at weekends when I was at school because this was where Father worked for Horace Griffin. Mrs Griffin's breeding stock was accredited and the eggs were sold for hatching to such people as Ewart

The old proverb, "if you want something done, ask a busy man" sums up John's attitude to life. His five years apprenticeship in the building trade has stood him in good stead; meticulous in his workmanship he has always had plenty to do. The village has benefited by his voluntary labour on many projects; but work has not distracted him from his love of sport; football, euchre, snooker, darts and vintage motorbikes, he enjoys them all.

Hebditch in Somerset. All the different breeding stock was kept in separate pens and the eggs sold for four times as much as they would make for table purposes. She kept a lot of ducks for table and she won many prizes with them. I stayed there for 15 months and then got a job with Mellets, timber merchants at Bigaton, Buckfastleigh where I could earn four times as much. I wanted to get in as an apprentice carpenter but there were no vacancies at that time. When a vacancy for an apprenticeship as a mason came up in 1950 with JWC Scoble at Kingsbridge I took it, I was then sixteen and a half. They were the main builders in those days employing about 120 men, many apprentices of all trades. My apprenticeship lasted until I was 21. The Government ruling was that you had to do five years after you started but they then brought in a rule that said you had to be paid by your age, and had to finish when you were 21 so I didn't quite complete five years.

I then did my National Service in 1955, I signed on as a Regular in the Royal Engineers mainly dealing with bridge building, mine clearing and that sort of thing. As I was a qualified builder my pay was a bit higher. We went to Worcester for a fortnight's basic training, square bashing and then moved on to Farnborough for twelve week's training. It was a bridge building camp plus mines and demolitions and all that type of thing. When I passed that I went abroad for two and half years to Tripoli in North Africa. We were within an armoured division with no infantry so we had to act as the infantry. It was desert warfare training and at that time there were about 10,000 of us out there.

In those days the firm you had worked with had to take you back for six months after you had finished your National Service. When I joined Scobles there were a 120 men but when I came back the Company was failing fast. The owner JWC Scoble had died and a management team ran the company. It was taken over a couple of times by different firms and there were virtually only half the men left. I don't know if I would have got sacked but some were being sacked every week. Nunns came along and I had already worked with one of them when I was learning my trade, he had been one of the top masons there.

Nunn's were originally carpenters only, and ladder makers in Church Street. Sometime in the mid 1950s they took on building as well and wanted masons. As I learned my trade with one of the brothers, Percy, who was a mason, he came and asked if I would work for them. Rather than stay with a dwindling firm I went on with them. There were three brothers, Wilf was a carpenter and dealt with the administration, Percy did the masonry and the youngest brother Alan, who later lived in Loddiswell, was also a carpenter. They were a sizeable company employing about 30 men. Like Alan Edgecombe they were taking on the trade, which Scobles had been loosing. There was also Lakemans of Aveton Gifford and then other firms started coming in like Rodgers of Holbeton.

When I was with Scobles in the 1950s we were building council houses; we built the first batch at Ashwood Park but Rodgers from Holbeton had the contract for the second lot. When I went with Nunns I was in charge of building the Roman Catholic Church at Salcombe and after I

left Nunns in 1963 and was working on my own, they 'phoned me up and asked if I would build the one at Modbury, because they wanted the same chaps to do it but I declined.

When I started Basil Taylor joined me and within a year we had a part time retired chap who helped, and after that we took on Ned Lethbridge full time. We built several houses and bungalows around here.

Reg. We were talking earlier about apprenticeships when a levy had to be paid to the government.

John. Not when I was an apprentice; it started in the early 1960s and by the 1980s the government had a scheme, the Construction Industry Training Board, (CITB) which paid an employer £50 a week for each apprentice and this came from the levy which everyone in the building trade had to pay whether you had an apprentice or not. It worked on a percentage of turnover; it cost quite a bit per year, it cost us up to about £180 a quarter.

Reg. In the 1960s Avon Farmers employed about 25 men in the building section and they had to pay thousands of pounds in levy, a part came back for the apprentices they employed.

John. Of course, some of the levy went towards Technical College training, you see, they had to go to college one day a week and the employer had to forfeit a day's pay. It was a good thing really but it didn't work all that well as it penalised small firms like ours who didn't get anything back. The scheme is still going, not only for apprentices but also for improvers. The problem now is that the apprentices have to be paid too much money. When I was an apprentice boy the pay was minimal for the first two years, by the third year you were getting about a third of a fully qualified man's pay. In the fourth year there was quite a big rise because you were becoming quite useful.

Reg. Does this account for some young people not wanting to take up the apprenticeship but starting as labourers and learning from that end, because they get a bit more pay that way.

John. You couldn't learn from that end really, well not originally, as you were a labourer only. The apprenticeships had almost died out, firstly a lot didn't want to take the job on, as it wasn't enough money. Then the Unions were fighting for the apprentice boys and got the pay up a bit and the bosses couldn't see the logic of employing them, as for the first couple of years they were losing out on the job. After training an apprentice the firm hoped they would stay on for the firm to get some benefit from their training, but at that time self-employment came in and, like us, many started on their own, we were one of the first in the area. Before that self-employment was non-existent, everyone worked for a firm where a tradesman in 1963 would earn £14/8/6- in a 48-hour week.

In 1961 Joan and I were married, her Father, Alan Luscombe lived at South Pool. He was good with mechanics, and lived and farmed down near the bridge at Mill Farm. Scoble Farm was the family farm, which ran right down to the point opposite Salcombe, and when the other brothers left her Uncle Percy farmed it.

Reg. Robert and Kevin were both born in Loddiswell?

John. Yes they were born in 1961 and 1964 and went to Loddiswell and then Kingsbridge schools. On leaving school Robert went to work for John Baxter, builder, who did a lot of work in Loddiswell. Then he went to work for Bert Taylor who was building some nice developments around the area. Robert began with him when they were building Oakwood Park, then Robert came with me and has been with me for many years. Kevin went as a technical electrical designer with a firm operating opposite the Regal Club in Kingsbridge. They did designs for electrical power stations and big projects like that. When the company left the area Kevin came building with us.

Reg. Robert and Kevin couldn't have had a better tutor.

John. You are only as good as the chap that teaches you, probably better sometimes; 'cause anybody with any sense will take the best of everything they are taught. The boys and I have worked together for many years, we are able to do building and carpentry, but for specialised joinery we usually get that done for us. I can do the plumbing for a whole house but usually we

Above: John with sons Robert and Kevin repairing the Church roof. 1999

Below: Rebuilding the Pavilion 1991. Left to Right. Kevin, Robert and John Webber, Reg Sampson, Rodney Brooking (builders). Bill Rockey (painter) Andy Guard (architect). Front row. Dennis Sharland, Betty Sampson, Ken Hyne (painters).

are too busy and it is far better to get a qualified plumber who has all the tools at hand and can do the job quicker.

In the old days it was all galvanised or copper pipes and then polythene and plastic pipes were brought in. Over the years the sizes kept changing from the old standard sizes to metric, there were about ten different sizes and about four different sizes for half inch. To get the fitting to join a pipe that's been in for 30 years was a bliming fine job but the modern stuff now is a lot more compatible with the copper fittings. The trouble is now, there are so many rules and regulations, it makes life difficult. I'm past retiring age by miles but I don't intend to give up completely, I still do a bit now and again.

Reg. During the years you have helped with many voluntary projects in the village.

John. Yes, we virtually rebuilt the Playing Field pavilion in 1991, the wooden walls had deteriorated and the place needed re-roofing. We built a concrete leaf all the way round, re-roofed and fitted new windows and doors. My two boys Robert and Kevin helped with Rodney Brooking, Andy Guard and, of course you and me. It cost us quite a few thousand pounds then. The pavilion is ideal for the Football Club, which I ran, either as Secretary or Treasurer for fourteen years when I was playing. After quite a long lapse I have now become involved again and regularly cut the pitch. The Club has had good sides and some poor ones especially in 1971 and 1972 when there was a shortage of players and we came out of the League for a year. The really best years have been since I packed up and when both my boys were playing, we won cup after cup. We had six or seven brilliant years in the Combination League in the 1960s. Then we decided to go into the South Devon League, which all the local clubs were in, and we had to start at the bottom, we were too good for them and often won 10-0. Then we went up a division every year and now we have been in Division One for four years where we are about holding our own, which is pretty good for a small village.

Another project has been the renovation of the Well for the Millennium. First we had to move 90

Above: The stone laid to commemorate Lod's Well. Below: The completed Lod's Well. "Another project has been the renovation of the Well for the Millennium. First we had to move 90 tons of soil and rubble, which had accumulated there over many years."

tons of soil and rubble, which had accumulated there over many years. Four of us did the work, Russell Baker, an engineer, Bill Penwill who had been used to working earth moving equipment and you and me. Now the project is finished it's well worth it, but I had my doubts at the time especially when we found we couldn't lift the water any higher. It eventually worked out very well and looks very good.

I like playing snooker, darts and euchre. The pubs found it difficult to get together a darts team so I play at the Sloop Inn, Bantham where there are about 14 of us. The Loddiswell Euchre Team which played at the New Bridge Inn now play at the Regal Club, Kingsbridge and snooker is played at the British Legion. Loddiswell had a good three-quarter-size snooker table in the Men's Club, which is now part of the Village Hall. When I went in the Army the Club folded up and the table was sold to the Portlemouth Youth Club for £40. A few years ago when their Club closed it was offered back to me for £100. I had it renovated and it is now in store.

Another hobby I have is restoring vintage motorbikes. I now have four bikes; they are an Ariel Fieldmaster, a Matchless G5 and two Bantam Supers. I ride to rallies and display them at Loddiswell Show along with a dozen or 15 other enthusiasts.

Reg. *Joan was always interested in sport.*

John. She's out nearly all the time! Years ago she played hockey for the Kingsbridge Ladies, and tennis for Kingsbridge and Loddiswell. Now she plays for the South Hams Indoor Bowling Team at the Sports Centre Kingsbridge. It is good we both have plenty to do.

Left; The loddiswell Show 1998 'my friend Russell Baker with the vintage motorbikes'

Vintage motorbikes in the village.
Bill Penwill has a BSA Gold Star,
Russell Baker a Norton 16 H and Norton 19,
Douglas Tarr a Triumph Tiger 90,
Graham Hodge an Ariel Fieldmaster and a Triumph Tiger 90,
Roger Eastley a BMW Tiger CZ,
Andy Pettitt a Harley Davidson,
Ian Hyne a BSA and a Triumph,
David Wallis a AJS model 18,
Michael Jarvis a Triumph Tiger 100 and John Marsh a BSA Gold Flash. Newer bikes are owned by Derek Hine and Chris Rogers.

Graham Hodge

Reg. I've come to a beautiful spot this morning, it is the Old Rectory along Station Road, and am looking across the Avon valley, to what used to be Rake Quarry, now replanted with shrubs and trees. It is the home of Graham and Ann Hodge. How long have you lived here?

Graham. We came back to the village in 1982 after living in Modbury where Ann Moysey and I were married and we had lived there for 20 years. I had an electrical contractors business there when we saw this place was for sale. I went to the auction and fortunately there weren't too many people bidding for it and I was lucky. It was then 'The Rectory' and was built in 1958 and had been empty for a few years. The Rev. Summerell was the first to live here and he was followed by the Rev Tyler in 1968.

When the Rev. Law was installed in 1977 he was in charge of four parishes and lived at Halwell so this Rectory was not wanted.

Reg. You originally lived in Loddiswell many years ago?

Graham. I was born in Towns Lane in April 1936 and when I was about three or four I often went into Jim and Annie Pedrick's

Childhood memories of his home life were centred on his Mother, Gladys, as his Father was in the Territorials, so was called up in 1939. She was fun loving and enjoyed participating in the Loddiswell plays and pantomimes. The cast were often reduced to tears of laughter by Betty Lethbridge's and her interpretation of the script. Graham gives a vivid account of his early life in the village and after doing his National Service in the Royal Electrical Engineers, returned to his trade as an electrician.

next door: I used to go in there quite a lot. The country was in a bit of a state and I remember hearing about the tons of shipping that were sunk, I clearly remember that.

My Father, Jack Hodge, was a shoemaker and lived in Kingsbridge; he lost his Father, that's my Grandfather, in the First World War. He was killed on the last day of the war and so Father had to give up shoemaking and went to work for Bill Noyce, a scrap metal merchant in Kingsbridge. He was in the Territorial Army so was called up in 1939, at the beginning of the war into the Devons and then into the 6th Airborne Division. He went into France by boat in a relief column to relieve Pegasus Bridge, you see, the first group had gone in at six in the morning. I have heard some tales but some were not very pleasant. He was demobbed in 1946 and went back to Bill Noyce's for a while. Sadly he had a kidney disease and died in 1956.

My Mother, Gladys, always had a part in the Plays written and produced by Miss Michell, and put on stage in Loddiswell, Kingsbridge and elsewhere: she enjoyed it.

Above: The Puritans at the 500th. Anniversary of Kingsbridge Fair. 1961. Left to Right. standing Roy Scobell, Michael Hine, Ethel Eva Hine, Nell Scobell, Leonard Scobell, sitting Dennis Hine, Emma Freeman, Ethel Hine and Gladys Hodge, (Graham's Mother).

Reg. Your young days were spent in Loddiswell?

Graham. Yes, as a young man in Town's Lane. I remember when the German bombers used to come over and we would walk up to Village Cross and see the red glow over Plymouth. Then back to bed about midnight unless bombs were dropped near the village.

Our games were soldiers, guns, that's what kids played with. We played football in the streets; there were hardly any cars about then. Sometimes we would go down to the copse below Great Gate, above New Mill and build 'shanties', quite a crowd of us, boys and girls together, we had a fine time. Mother didn't worry about us, she said, "When Torr Quarry blasts at one o'clock I expect you to be home". We always knew what the time was, we could tell the time by the train. Bob Hine was a engine driver whose Mother lived in Loddiswell, he would blow his whistle, so there was no excuse to be home late.

When I was four I went to Miss Michell's class in the Village Hall so that Mother could go to work, it was war time. She was in charge of the telephone exchange in the Post Office, taking all the messages and plugging them through. There were telegrams when someone was wounded or killed and I used to get sixpence to take it out to Woolston, Stanton or wherever and a penny-halfpenny for the village. Most of the time telegrams were bad news.

When I went to the Secondary Modern school at

Kingsbridge we went on the train as the school bus was overcrowded and for the last two years they wouldn't put on a bigger bus. There were three of us, Tony Hyne, Vivien Hine and myself, it would have been nearly as well to walk to Kingsbridge, by the time we walked to the station and then from Kingsbridge station to school in Fosse Road.

I played football right through from when I was eleven years old, I captained the school football team and played rugby and quite enjoyed it. That led on later to playing for Loddiswell football team, which started in Robin's Park and then up at Village Cross in Sid Brooking's field. I was also encouraged to play rugby for Kingsbridge by my Father because he used to play for them.

On Sunday mornings we went to Sunday School and in the afternoons, still in our best clothes, would go for a walk often up the railway line and through Sorley Tunnel picking wild strawberries on the way. There were no trains on Sundays so we could get on the ganger's trolley and paddle it up and down the line. We could go up as far as the tunnel and 'didn't we travel coming down round Rake! Boys of all ages used to mix together in those days.

There were some old stories told in those days. A number of young people used to travel to Kingsbridge by train and in the dark winter evenings they said there was a ghost in Well Street that they met on the way home from the station. They were frightened out of their wits, as this object would chase them up the road. It went on for ages and they wouldn't come that way, in fact, they got in such a state they had to be escorted through.

Eventually a crowd of boys said enough was enough so they laid in wait for this so called ghost and they found it was a young chap called Bassett under a sheet. It was only a prank but he kept it going for some time. It was wartime and we had heard of German parachutists dropping in.

I remember the chaps that came back from Dunkirk were stationed in the Congregational Hall and Phyllis Elliott used to do the washing for Ern Robinson, she later became Mrs Robinson. Then we had the Yanks here in 1943;

their main vitualling base was at Loddiswell Station and we boys used to walk down; they gave out tins of peaches, they were very generous really and the pubs did very well too. The village was choc-a-bloc with trucks and jeeps in the evenings; there was hardly room to walk.

I left school at 15 but the year before one could leave at fourteen years old. I was quite upset they changed it, as I wanted to go down to the concrete works where I could earn more money.

My Father said I should learn a trade first and then, if I wanted, I could go down there. So I did an apprenticeship as an electrician with Scoble's, the builders in Wallingford Road. That took me five years, they had a 100 men working

Below: Graham's Father, Jack in the Devon's and then the 6th. Airborne Division 1940 "He went into France by boat in a relief column to relieve Pegasus Bridge..."

for them then. I had 28 shillings a week and had to provide my overalls and tools, and give Mother a bob or two for my keep.

My electrical knowledge had started with Sid Jeffery on Saturday mornings; he was a very talented man with clocks and watches and he showed me how to charge up accumulators for people's wireless sets, I had to connect them all up.

I was conscripted in 1956 and joined the Royal Electrical and Mechanical Engineers (REME) in Blandford, Dorset and I was in for two years. When I joined up I had ten shillings and sixpence a week so I couldn't do a lot with that. I did six weeks basic training, square bashing and route marching. We didn't think much of it at the time but looking back on it the whole training was a good experience. They were a nice bunch of lads, honest and trustworthy, not like the situation now.

Then I went on a Trade Course at Gosport, Hampshire, but then unfortunately my Father died so I had a compassionate posting to Yeovil, a bit nearer home. I was able to travel up and down on my motorbike on a 24-hour pass to see my Mum and Ann, my fiancée, whom I had known since 1953.

In R.E.M.E my work was on the electrics in vehicles, which was very useful to me, it didn't expand my trade a lot as I was used to house wiring but it broadened my knowledge for later in life. I did repairs on the electrics on motorcycles, which is handy now with all the vintage bikes in Loddiswell. They had magnetos like the tractors but later coil ignition was more generally used.

I suppose we must have got 15 or more vintage bikes now in the village, they are really nice machines. I've got an Ariel 500 Twin made in 1955 and I wouldn't mind another one to do up.

Below: "I was conscripted in 1956 and joined the Royal Electrical and Mechanical Engineers (REME) in Blandford, Dorset" Graham is on the back row far left of the picture.

Cliff and Priscilla Bye

Reg. We are very fortunate in Loddiswell parish that many people have come to live in the area and have made a valuable contribution to society generally and Col. Clifford Bye and his wife Priscilla are no exceptions. Which year did you come to Loddiswell and why did you choose to live here?

Cliff. We bought New Mill in December 1984; we had been looking for a new home. We were living in Twickenham and we had connections of very long standing with the West Country, so we looked here for a retirement residence. Quite by chance we found the house particulars among our documents when we came down to do some house hunting. We stayed at the Soar Mill Cove Hotel at the time.

We found this property was for auction; Priscilla's sister was visiting us from East Devon so we guided her back through Loddiswell to the main road. We stopped to look at New Mill, it was a glorious summer evening and we returned the next day and fell in love with it.

Reg. I quite believe you could, it is a beautiful mill, right here beside the river Avon.

Cliff and Priscilla came into the parish on their retirement and have contributed greatly to the community. Cliff's valued opinion has helped in decision making on the Parish Council, School Governors and the PCC.

They have welcomed many organisations to meetings at The Mill. The Church Fete has been held in the lovely riverside gardens for many years. Life before retirement was dominated by responsibility and travel. Their stories give an insight into life in the Services and Priscilla's experiences of Colonial days, now a thing of the past.

Priscilla. We had connections with the previous owner.

Cliff. Yes, when we were purchasing the house we found we had connections with the previous owner, Mr. Kitsell.

He had been in the Far East a great deal of his life as a tin mining engineer and we discovered we had lots of places in common which we knew. We then realised that he knew Priscilla's Mother because he had a collection of over a hundred Staffordshire figures and a tapestry made by all the ladies who were incarcerated in Changi Jail in the war in Singapore. She remembered all this too and spoke of it. The story was that Mr. Kitsell was captured in the war, but fortunately his wife was back in the UK. In the end we agreed a price and bought New Mill.

Reg. Since retiring you have become involved with many organisations and often provided the venue for the Church Fete.

Cliff. We have three children and each of them have three children of their own, so we have been a haven for nine grandchildren who love being here and running around the place, fishing for tiddlers in the river and that sort of thing. It has been a great place for the family but now they are growing up and we are getting older so we are looking to the future.

*Reg. **One of the family has opened the Fete for us!***

Cliff. Yes, Ruby Wax, who is married to our son, Ed. She had rather a hectic time, flying back from America, coming down on the train in time to open the Fete in the afternoon.

*Reg. **Of course Ed is known for his production of 'Red Dwarf' and many others.***

Priscilla. Yes, he's about to direct his second film.

Cliff. He has been a television director and producer all his working life and he met Ruby because he was assigned to direct one of her sequences. They hadn't met before but by the end of the production they were engaged to be married. Now they have a son and two daughters.

Priscilla. She thought he was too young to be a director.

*Reg. **One of the family lives in France?***

Cliff. Our younger daughter, Joanna, is married to a Frenchman, Jean-Francois Le Borgne, a French Government official promoting overseas trade, and they have three children, two boys and a girl. They live about 30 miles outside Paris on the north-west side in a village called Mavrecourt and they come down to visit us a great deal. Our elder daughter, Julia, is married to Spencer Canning and they have two girls and a boy. She is a freelance book editor.

*Reg. **You were a colleague of mine on the Parish Council and the School Governors.***

Cliff. It was about seven or eight years on the Council, As far as the Church Parochial Council is concerned, it is 17 years.

*Reg. **You mentioned Twickenham was your previous home.***

Cliff. That was our last home before we moved here, but we've had a large number of homes all over the world.

Priscilla. We've had 32 homes!

*Reg. **Your involvement with the Royal Marines, (RM) must have taken you to different places!***

Cliff. I joined the Marines straight from School

Below: New Mill. 1930 "...we found we had connections with the previous owner, Mr. Kitsell... he knew Priscilla's mother."

and was commissioned on 1st January 1941. I did 18 months training in a batch of eleven Second Lieutenants, which culminated in three months in the Tactical School at the Thurlestone Hotel, which had been commandeered as a RM Training Centre. Incidentally this gave me my only ride on the South Brent-Kingsbridge railway, there and back.

Reg. You must have had some war experiences?

Cliff. I joined HMS Duke of York in July 1942 and served in her until November 1944. She was one of our five most modern battleships of which HMS Prince of Wales was sunk off Singapore. We were based in Scapa Flow for a large part of our time covering Russian Convoys in case German heavy ships attacked.

In December 1943 we were engaged in the sinking of the German battleship Scharnhorst in pitch darkness off North Cape, Norway. We had 18 survivors on board and in a recent TV programme about the action the survivors appeared! I recognised one of them! It was a very eerie experience! Earlier we had gone to the Mediterranean to help support the 1st Army landings in North Africa.

After I left the ship I joined the Commandos, I was trained at Achnacarry in Scotland. For a short time I was an instructor there and then I joined 1st Commando Brigade in Germany and was posted to 46 Commando RM. We returned to UK to train and re-equip to take part in the re-conquest of Singapore and Malaya. However, the atomic bombs were dropped, the war was ended and 46 Commando was disbanded in UK in 1945.

I went on to do a specialisation course in Communications for 18 months covering the army, naval and combined operations. After this I was posted to the west country to run a small Signals Tactical wing, and simultaneously acted as a Signals Officer to the Commando School, the Officer's School and the General's HQ at Plymouth. I lived on a motorbike! Then I joined the Officer's School full time in Stonehouse Barracks, Plymouth as an instructor of young officers, shades of the Thurlestone Hotel.

While I was in Plymouth I met Priscilla whose family lived at Crapstone, between Yelverton and Tavistock. It happened because a friend called Henry Evington had been an engineer officer in the Duke of York. He had been appointed on the staff at the College at Manadon and invited me to a party there. He also asked Priscilla and that's how we first met. We were married at Buckland Monachorum Church in 1951.

After a short honeymoon we went off to our first posting as a married couple, by troopship to Singapore, up to Ipoh in Malaya (now Malaysia) by air, to join HQ 3 Commando Brigade as Brigade Signals Officer. The brigade was operating in the State of Perak against Communist infiltration. Then the brigade moved to Malta where we readjusted ourselves to amphibious operations under the eagle eye of the Commander-in-Chief, Mediterranean, Admiral Lord Louis Mountbatten. However, we were flown at short notice, to the Canal Zone in Egypt. Priscilla was left in Malta with all the families. In 1954 my time was up, Priscilla flew home with our new-born daughter, Julia, and I followed from Egypt.

Reg. This was before the Suez crisis?

Cliff. Yes, that was in 1956 when I attended the Army Staff College. Subsequently I was on the staff of the Major-General in Plymouth before being promoted to Major, and moved to the Ministry of Defence (MOD) on the staff of the Commandant-General, Royal Marines, as an amphibious warfare planner, mainly concerned with the conversion of HMS Bulwark into a Commando ship. It was an extremely interesting job that broke new ground in many ways.

Then I became the Chief Signals Officer, Royal Marines, and followed this by being a member of a travelling lecture team through the USA and to Hong Kong. It was glorious fun but I was then brought down to earth by being made Second-in-Command of 40 Commandos. We were based in Johore Bahru but operated in North Borneo with the British Army to help counter the Indonesian Confrontation. We came and went on four or five months tours by Commando Ships.

Then in 1966-67 I commanded 45 Commando

RM, operating in Aden and South Yemen to help counter terrorism and enable the UK Forces to withdraw in orderly fashion from Aden Colony. Priscilla was at home in Crapstone where we had our own home. I left 45 Commando shortly before the final withdrawal but was recalled after two weeks leave (it should have been three months) to assist in the planning details for the final withdrawal.

I then returned to the MOD as a planner in the Department of CGRM and moved over to the Naval Staff in the Directorate of Naval Warfare.

Finally I was appointed to the Commando Training Centre at Lympstone as Commandant where I had two and a half years of extremely exciting and enjoyable life, not only running the major military training centre in the area but also integrating with the local people and activities in general. It used to give me enormous pleasure to watch the recruit squads passing out of Lympstone as trained commandos wearing their green berets. What gave me most reward was when so many families came up to me after the ceremony was over to say how much they appreciated the wonderful way in which the Marines had developed their young men and made them into what they were. That, of course, made the whole thing worthwhile.

Reg. What was your rank then?

Cliff. By then I was a Colonel and I retired with that rank in 1972.

I got my first civil job as a member of the personnel staff of Grindlays Bank in the city of London; Grindlays had been the British bank used by the expatriates in India. My job was Group Training Manager and I was responsible for the development and training of the staff, not only in London but also by liaison with all the branches of the Bank from USA to Hong Kong. I had a lot of travelling to do in the Middle East and Indian subcontinent.

Reg. Your experience in communications was useful there?

Cliff. Yes it was and in the course of this I was fortunate to retrace the steps that Priscilla had taken years before, and I was able to see for myself what she had so often described to me.

Above: Commandant at the Commando Training Centre, Lympstone. 1970 "... I had two and a half years of extremely exciting and enjoyable life there."

While I was at Grindlays I was given the opportunity to take on a new job, I was the only Englishman in the French Peugeot Car Company based on Lagos and Kaduna in Nigeria. My job was to run the training and development of the staff and to act as a communication link between the French and Nigerians who, of course, spoke English; I was in fact the only Englishman there. There were seventy Frenchman and four and a half thousand Nigerians. This was a fantastic job in a new part of the World for us altogether. It was pretty tough from a living point of view, but we arrived back eventually, none the worse for our experience and very much richer for it too. We had five homes in Nigeria, in Lagos and Kaduna. During the time we were out there we still had a home in Twickenham on the Green and that's where our three children lived while we were abroad. Edward, for example, developed his television and production training, Julia was working in publishing and Jo worked locally with an estate agent, the three of them ran the house. We came home for a month's holiday once a year during the time we were in Nigeria. When we returned from Nigeria I did a job for a couple of years as a Director for a Personnel Management Consultancy. When that was over we decided we would move down to Devon. We arrived here in December 1984.

Reg. I have an affinity with this Mill as my Grandfather, that is my Mother's father, was born here in 1862? Priscilla, in your young days what did you know of this area?

Priscilla. I was born in Devon and lived in Penlee Gardens, Stoke, Devonport. My Father, a Scot, was in the Royal Navy. He became an Engineer-Rear-Admiral but died sadly when I was quite young. I have an elder sister who was in the Women's Royal Naval Service (WRNS) and married into the Navy. My brother was also in the Navy and specialised in Naval Aviation.

Reg. Was this about 1941?

Priscilla. Yes, I was at school during the war, first at Moorfield in Plymouth and then boarding school at West Heath, evacuated to Claydon House, Buckinghamshire. Canadians camped nearby, we were told to ignore them, difficult! Back at home in Stoke we were badly placed for bombs between Plymouth and Devonport. We had a land mine in the little back garden and another in the front of the house. Shrapnel fell on my pillow; we had many air-raids and sheltered in a converted coal cellar under the house. I had measles and we spent a few days in Widecombe for me to recover. A friend rang my Mother and said "Sorry about your house!" which was completely flat. We bicycled into Stoke from Widecombe, quite a feat, to see the ruins.

Reg. It must have been very traumatic!

Priscilla. Yes, my Mother was wonderful and found various homes in Widecombe, Chudleigh, in Cornwall and eventually shared a friend's house at Cleeve, Ivybridge until the end of the War. We used to entertain American soldiers stationed at Ivybridge before they went off on D Day and many were sadly lost.

After school I went to Atholl Crescent, Domestic Science College in Edinburgh, sharing digs with a school friend, Rosemary Colville. Her Father was the Governor of Bombay Province so Rosemary and I went to India to help! Bombay was the first province so when The Viceroy was very busy Rosemary's Father took over. It happened that her Father and Mother were in Delhi when we arrived, Wavell, the then Viceroy, was away. Life was quite a change from digs in Edinburgh. Later Mountbatten was The Viceroy and we went to Delhi and Poona, the summer retreat, quite often. Life was very spoiling; in Delhi the corridors were alive with staff dressed in splendid red and white uniform. We dined in splendour with fascinating visitors, always in evening dress, and the ladies retired from the table first by walking backwards before

Below: Priscilla on a shooting expedition in the Punjab 1947 The grass is called Tiger Grass and is 15 ft tall! "Life was quite a change from digs in Edinburgh."

curtsying at the door, hopefully without falling over.

In Bombay and Delhi we would be up at six am to ride and exercise the horses on Bombay Racecourse, and in Delhi, on ground so hard that we were told not to fall off as it would be lethal. Every day we had plans given for the day and we also helped with local charities. We went to many places in Bombay Province and elsewhere, particularly in Poona. Whenever the Viceroy or his wife appeared we had to curtsy. Once I remember being in the swimming pool and sinking in a curtsy under water!

We were in Bombay during the troubles of the Partition between the Hindus and Moslems with a great number of deaths, very sadly. On my return from India my sister and I looked after my Mother who had a hip operation, which took seven months in plaster from waist to feet in those days!

In 1951 I met Cliff at a party at Manadon at the Royal Naval Engineering College. We married and went instantly to Ipoh in Malaya. I became Secretary to the Chief Police Officer of Perak, Mr Gaffiking. They must have been desperate as I am a rotten speller and couldn't type. He was a very kind man and I learned a lot.

We went to Malta where Julia was born, Cliff was in the Canal Zone in Egypt. Later in Johore Bahru in Malaya with three children by then, Cliff was mostly in Borneo. I ran the Service's Youth Club for Singapore and Johore Bahru in Malaya (previous experience nil). I also ran the Johore Bahru Girl Guides (previous experience, one term at school).

After our retirement from the Royal Marines we lived in Twickenham. Cliff was with Grindlay's Bank and I had a variety of jobs with a friend, including driving cars for Brentford Car Auctioneers, and running the King George's Fund for Sailors in Twickenham. Then we went to Nigeria with the Peugeot Car Company, living in Lagos and Kaduna. It was an amazing experience and we made many friends of different nationalities. Eventually we came to Devon and live in this Old Mill with our bulldog. We have both very much enjoyed being involved in local affairs in the area.

Below: Cliff thanking the author, Mary Wesley, for opening the Church Fete at New Mill. 1995

Ivor and Joan King with Rachael Tate

Reg. Your house is called Vareoak, how did the name originate?

Joan. Our Deeds go back to 1700 when Thomas King owned the land, which was called Vareoak so we kept the name. I don't think there is any relationship. You see Ivor's family came from Sidbury.

Reg. Did your family always live in Loddiswell?

Joan. My Mother, Sheelah Taylor, was born in London, her Mother was born in Stornaway, she went to London as a nurse and there met my Grandfather, Walter John Guest, who was from Loddiswell. He was born in 1886; he left school at the age of nine to go on the Stage Coach with his brother, Lewis Guest, who drove the coach from Torcross to Dartmouth. Later he went to London at the age of 19 to work in the clothing and furniture business. His health was not good as he suffered with breathing problems and, when in hospital, he met Joan Mary McCleod who later became his wife. She became the Parish Nurse in Loddiswell and was presented with a gold engraved watch for her

Joan and Rachael's entrepreneurial Grandfather, Walter Guest, started the business, which the family continued to develop into a highly successful enterprise. The South Hams Packing Station provided employment for many in the area. The changing pattern of farming influenced the way they adapted. Eventually the business was impeded by intolerable and unnecessary European Economic Community legislation making the business uneconomic. Their Grandmother, Nurse Guest was a very popular lady, always willing to deal with emergencies and maternity care.

services from 1914 to 1927 from the Loddiswell Nursing Association. She died in 1940 aged 63, from a severe angina attack after attending a soldier who had cut his finger.

On my Grandfather's return to Loddiswell he began a Carriers business to Plymouth with two horses and a wagon, a journey of seven hours each way. He would leave Loddiswell on a Friday morning and return on Saturday night.

During the 1914 to 1918 War he was the first person in the village to own a van, it was a Fiat with solid tyres. He used to take the mail from Kingsbridge to Totnes and also helped his brother Lewis, with his Carriers business at Torcross with the van. One of the jobs he did was to take the Monks from Wood Barton to Exeter on their journey back to France in 1921. I remember my Mother saying the Bibles took four men to lift them. He left for that journey at four in the morning.

My Grandfather started to collect butter and eggs from the farms in 1911 and eventually he started to buy the milk from the farmers, saving them the work of making butter. He took the milk to Torquay, serving Totnes and Paignton on the way. The bulk of the milk went to the Torquay Co-operative and he was the first man to buy milk direct from the farms in the South Hams.

In 1918 after his Mother's death he bought the New Bridge Inn, which he ran in addition to the milk business. The Milk Marketing Board was set up in 1933, and then he had to take the milk to the Cow and Gate Factory at Totnes, which later became Unigate. That continued for many years taking the milk churns every day until the tankers came in. Both businesses continued until his death at the age of 57 in 1943. His daughters, Sheelah Taylor (my Mother) and her

Below: Jack and Nurse Guest, Grandparents "My Mother, Sheelah Taylor, was born in London, her Mother was born in Stornaway, she went to London as a nurse and there met my Grandfather, Walter John Guest."

sister Iris Wallbutton continued the egg and poultry business until 1983.

My Father, Wilfred Taylor, was born at Preston Cottages, Woodleigh and had three brothers and one sister. On Sundays they had to go to Moreleigh Church three times a day, morning service, Sunday school and the evening service. They went to school at Woodleigh and he left at the age of fourteen to work at Torr Quarry using a fourteen-pound hammer to break the stones. His Mother, Maria, used to walk down Yeo Lane to Topsham Bridge and up to Coombe Cross taking rabbits and chickens to sell to someone who paid two shillings (ten pence) for the chickens.

Rachael. Mother first met Father when she was going to Knowles Hill Grammar School in Newton Abbot, they used to wave to each other when she was on the train. Mother and her two sisters all won scholarships and went to school at Newton Abbot.

Reg. **Where were you born, Joan?**

Joan. I was born at No 12. The Bank in 1940, so did not know much about the war. We lived next door to the Devon Constabulary where P C Jane lived. When the evacuation of the Torcross area took place in 1943 our Great Uncle Lewis Guest, who used to drive the coach and horses from Torcross to Dartmouth moved in.

Rachael. By that time Father was driving one of the lorries from the business down in Cornwall when they built the Davidstow aerodrome, so he was away during the week. When he was away, Mother used to take us down to the New

Below: South Hams Egg Packing Station, Loddiswell. 1952

Bridge Inn when there was a raid on Plymouth. I can still remember being in Kingsbridge when it was bombed. Roger, our brother, was in the cinema at the time and I was at the top of the town when a bomb fell on the other side of the street. This was about 1943 when I was five.

During and after the war the egg and poultry business continued to develop and by the 1950s battery hens and broilers were being kept in larger numbers.

A new Packing Station was built in the Courtledge, a nice roomy building. By that time we employed 35 people, about 30 on the egg grading and poultry processing and five men out collecting. We collected in the area from nearly 1,000 customers during the week.

By the late sixties the smaller farmers gave up their hens and by the mid 1970s we were only collecting from about ten large producers. We went twice a week to all of them and we were picking up as many eggs as we were previously collecting from a thousand customers. These producers had many thousands of hens, one or two with 10,000.

We also had our own production unit because when a large producer cleared their old hens, suddenly the egg sales side was short. By having our own unit we could balance the supply. The eggs were sold locally but the bulk of them were sold to Stewart's at Southampton, Poole, Brighton and Hove. They came twice a week to collect the eggs, later we sent them direct into London at Tooley Street.

Reg. What happened to the processed hens?
Rachael. They were sold mainly locally to the butchers and we also sold chicken to Sainsburys who required chicken from the South Hams area. We processed them and sent them by train,

Below: Ivor processing chicken for market at the Poultry Packing Station. 1964

Below: Joan, brother Roger and Rachael at their trade stand at Kingsbridge Show. "We also supplied the Royal Yacht Britannia with chicken for the Queen, when she was visiting the Dartmouth Royal Naval College."

while hens went to Smithfield Market. We also supplied the Royal Yacht Britannia with chicken for the Queen, when she was visiting the Dartmouth Royal Naval College.

Reg. It was a good business! Why did you give it up?

Rachael. As far as the milk business was concerned, the bulk tankers were collecting the milk so that business was gone. In the late 1970s new rules and regulations were introduced from Europe which imposed a rule that a Veterinary Surgeon had to be present all the time we were processing. Inspections from the Health Authorities would be required twice a week and all the equipment had to be brought up to new European standards. This would have meant spending between £50,000 and £75,000 to bring the equipment up to date, as well as the cost of a vet. We did not feel the margin of profit would justify the outlay.

We closed the business in 1983. During the time we were in business we bought frozen food from N C Roach and Son, Cornwall and when we decided to close Graham Roach bought out the frozen side of our Company and took over all the customers. As Roger, our brother, Joan and I knew the business so well he asked us if we would go to Newton Abbot where he was developing a new branch of Roach Foods. Roger was a Representative, selling frozen foods, bacon and gammons, which later became their biggest product, in fact now the largest in the country.

Reg. Danish?

Rachael. No, when we first started with Roach's father they sold Dutch, but when they took over the Dalehead Company, who produced a lot of pigs, then they could supply English Bacon.

In 2001 they were processing in the region of 50,000 pigs a week. Joan and I were with Roach Foods for 18 years until we retired in 2001.

Reg. What are your interests now?

Joan. Grandchildren are my main interest but I will no doubt find something to occupy me. I am interested in the local Charities. Mother was appointed a Feoffee of the Arundell and Philips Charities in 1970 and I was appointed in 1986. The Arundell Charity was bequeathed by the Lord of the Manor, Sir Matthew Arundell of Hatch in 1591 and is "*for the good and behoof of the parishioners of Loddiswell.*" The Philips Charity was formed in 1728 by the gift of two farms by Richard Philips for the benefit of the poorer people of the village. This has now been changed to pensioners over 60 years of age and the distribution takes place on his tomb in the chancel on St. Stephen's Day.

Reg. When did you come to Loddiswell Ivor?

Ivor. That was in 1960; before that I lived in Bigbury village. I was offered a job at the Egg Packing Station, I suppose because I was courting one of the daughters, Joan. I did anything on the poultry side, collecting eggs; there are very few farms that I haven't visited in the South Hams. I would pick up hens at four in the morning for the processing plant or deliver eggs to Torquay and Plymouth areas two and three times a week. I did anything that was needed as anyone would in a family business.

I used to drive the milk lorry as a relief driver. In those days there were ten pickups from small farmers before I got to Loddiswell Butts. Most of them have disappeared and now there are only four in the area. When the business closed I was offered a position in a butcher's shop in Modbury but after a while my health wasn't so good and I had to retire.

Reg. You were married in 1963. What do you remember of that year?

Joan. That was the year of the blizzard. We were married on April 15th and when we left to go on our honeymoon there was still snow on the tops of the hedges, which had remained from the snow in early January. It was a bitterly cold few months.

Ivor. The milk lorry could not go for several days and I remember going out on a Monday evening to the bottom of Rings Lane to pick up churns in the van. A bulldozer had gone ahead to clear a track but when we got to Rings we could go no further and I had to reverse all the way back in the dark to Woolston Lodge in order to turn around. As I reversed there must have been a foot of water in the track and the next morning this was solid ice. It is a good thing that every year is not like that.

Sheila Elliott

Reg. I have come to talk this morning to Sheila Elliott at Oaklee in Oakwood Park. Could you tell me, Sheila, about the early days of the Courtledge when your Grandfather lived there?

Sheila. Yes, I suppose so. My Grandparents lived at Park View, later called Lydiard Cottage. Grandfather, Richard West, had a horse and a pony, and was the carrier to Kingsbridge, he used to bring home all the goods. I remember Mother saying as a youngster she had to go out on the dark nights delivering goods. Her sister, Auntie Ethel was very nervous and she couldn't do it. He brought home anything, medicines and things like that. Mother was the only one to walk to Alleron and around to the various houses and farms to deliver.

In those days there were no cars in the Courtledge, just the pump there in the middle. We used to go out playing; even when our daughter, Jane, was born she was able to run free in the Courtledge. Several families lived around there, the Brookings, Pearl and all that family, Mrs Hine, Rene Preston, the Popplestones and Eastleys. The shop would have been Rosie Preston's and

Sheila's life has revolved around the village community. Her Father served in the navy in the First World War and was immediately called up at the beginning of the Second War when he experienced many lucky escapes. Sheila joined the Women's Royal Naval Service (WRNS) and after returning to civilian life married Owen. The family ran Elliott's bakery and grocery store, an important and vital service for the village, for the next 30 years.

the cottage adjoining was Miss Yalland's, Mrs Yabsley, who later lived there, was still over at Wyselands. I went to Loddiswell School; I was about ten when Miss Michell came and a year later Miss Common. She came after Mrs Foot, and Miss Todd was also there. Twelve months after that I went to Kingsbridge and I left there when I was fourteen. I went up with the Hallidays at the Cottage to help.

(General Sir Lewis Halliday with his wife Violet, retired to Loddiswell from the Royal Marines in 1930. He had been awarded the Victoria Cross for his defence of the British Legation in Peking in 1900)

My brother Gordon died of Multiple Sclerosis when he was 21 in January 1942; he was five years older than me.

Reg. I remember Gordon walking through the village with a limp and soon had a wooden wheel chair.

Sheila. There were always some boys to help push him around. Gordon would lead the boys on by staying outside the wall to whistle when the boys were scrumping apples, and he supervised the football.

My Father, Arthur Taylor, was in the Navy; he joined at the age of 15 although he gave his age

Above: Arthur Taylor, Sheila's Father. 1940

joining the Courageous, and they were promptly assigned to another ship.

It was a lucky drink as, within a short time HMS Courageous was torpedoed and sunk with a considerable loss of life. It was a little while before the family knew he was not on the aircraft carrier.

Later he was assigned to HMS Exeter at the time when the battleship Graf Spee slipped out of the Baltic to sail down to Montevideo on the River Plate to get to a neutral country for safety. It was chased by HMS Exeter, HMS Achilles and HMS Ajax, all of which were vulnerable to Graf Spee's heavy guns. Exeter was hit and severely damaged and so were the other two. Although she was chased and reached Montevideo in safety the Captain scuttled the Graf Spee in the mouth of the River Plate so that she couldn't be captured. Father missed all of this because soon after leaving port, Father was hurrying along the deck of the Exeter, tripped over a bucket and ruptured himself. He was taken off into hospital for an operation, and because the Exeter was believed to be lost it was assumed he was drowned. Although my Mother, Alice, felt convinced he was still alive the family had no

Below: Richard West, Grandfather, leaving Kingsbridge with his carrier wagon. 1902

as 17, the minimum age. He served through the First War as a Stoker and completed his 22 years of service before he retired back to Loddiswell. He developed a smallholding with cows, pigs and hens in Oakwood Park where Jimmy Middlewick previously had a smallholding. At the outbreak of the Second World War he was recalled as a stoker in 1940 to join HMS Courageous, an aircraft carrier. Fortunately, or unfortunately, he spent the previous evening at the New Bridge Inn with Frank Mabin who was also due to join the next day. The festivities took their toll and my Father and Frank missed

news of him for nearly nine months.

We went to London in the meantime, the three of us, Mother, Janet and I, and stayed with Mrs Morland where Auntie Nance was the housekeeper for quite a while. Gordon had died, but Father didn't know until he was on the way home. Eventually Mother and Janet came back but I stayed and helped a bit. There were a lot of Air Force chaps staying there at various times when they were on leave.

Then I decided I was going to join up and went into the Women's Royal Naval Service (WRNS). First they sent me to Scotland, Balloch near Loch Lomond in 1943, it was a lovely time of the year, it was July, beautiful.

I was there two years and when we came down I was stationed at East Meon, near Portsmouth at a signal station. We were coming to the end of the war and I was an Officer's Steward, very interesting. We used to see a lot of the Officers and then I was demobbed in 1945. I don't remember what I came home in, so I suppose I came home in uniform, but I probably did like Father always did, or so Mother said; he would take off his uniform and leave it trailing up the stairs.

When I came back to Loddiswell I worked at Powlesland's at the London House Stores. Tom Brooking was there at the time and when Bert and Owen Elliott were demobbed from the RAF they decided to go into the shop that was established by their Grandparents, William and Selina Elliott in 1888. I was 19 then and I joined them there.

Bert had worked as a mechanical engineer in charge of Aggett's Garage at Bovey Tracey before he was called into the RAF. Owen had also served in the RAF working on airframes and for three years he was stationed at an air base in the Transvaal in South Africa.

Owen and I were married in September 1950 when I was 24 and we lived with my Mum at Park View for two or three years after we were married. Then when Mrs Bush gave up the old Post Office Fred Diamond went there to live for a while.

When Fred went to Tyepitte Cottage we had the place refurbished and we moved in. So during the time we were in the business we were living in Fore Street. When we gave up the shop we went in the top cottage for nine months and Owen's brother Bert moved into the middle cottage next to the shop.

John Webber had bought a plot of land from Mrs Wallbutton in Well Street; and he said he was going to build houses there. We had one and called it Nanpara after Poldark, the series on television. I always liked that programme and I liked the name.

We were down there for ten years I suppose, and we tried for planning permission for this place a time or two and eventually got it and John Webber and Basil Taylor built it. We came here to Oaklee in 1986.

I helped in the bakery and grocery business for 30 years until we left and I was then 50 years old. I knew everybody then, but not now. The village has grown with new houses and many people have moved in. People go off to Plymouth to work and some you don't see very often.

Reg. How do you spend your leisure now Sheila?

Sheila. Looking after the grandchildren I suppose, often two and a half days a week when their parents are away at work and then we feed the whole family. When their parents go out for an evening the children say, " We'll go up to Nan's to sleep". They are always quite happy here.

Below: The Courtledge in 1930 "In those days there were no cars in the Courtledge, just the pump there in the middle."

Russell Baker

Reg. I am at Hazeltor this morning, the home of Russell and Jean Baker, it overlooks Great Gate Farm and right down the valley to the bridges over the Avon and the open ground right up to Churchstow, a lovely big open valley. How long have you lived here Russell?

Russell. We built this place ourselves with a bit of help from the professionals in 1967, having bought a bit of the field from Mr. Foss who lived in Glencairn alongside. We went out to Bigbury for three years and did a bit of speculative building after I sold the California Cross engineering business.

*Reg. **Where were you brought up?***

Russell. I was born in May 1929 and my Mother died in August when I was eight weeks old so I was brought up by my Grandparents at Higher Hazelwood Farm. My Father was Jack Baker and he was born at Crannacombe. When I was born he was living at Higher Sigdon and he had a threshing and contracting business.

*Reg. **Your early days were spent at Higher Hazelwood.***

Russell. My Father Jack was one of ten

Russell has been a craftsman all his life; from his early years his great love of engineering has stood him in good stead. Whatever the problem Russell would always find a solution, not only in tractor and implement repairs, but also in construction and ironwork. National Service in the RAF motivated his appetite for travel and in his retirement he and Jean have taken the opportunity to travel at home and abroad with their motorbike and sidecar.

children. There was Annie, Percy, Ethel, Henley, Bert, Jack, Fred, Dorothy, Mary and Alan. They were a farming family and did quite a lot of threshing and contracting, especially Henley and Alan. They had a partnership and did threshing in the Bigbury, Kingston, Ringmore and Modbury areas whereas Father covered the areas Loddiswell, Churchstow, Malborough and Salcombe. In fact, during the war they were allocated these areas. In those days the grain was bagged up and carried to the barn in the two cwt. West of England sacks, and if it was a bit damp shaken out on the floor to dry.

I went to school at Kingsbridge, down to Gara Bridge and on the train. There were five or six of us from Hazelwood and surrounding area. I was five years old and we had to make our way from Kingsbridge station to the Primary School in Belle Hill. In those days there was very little traffic and we walked as a group.

*Reg. **Were you always interested in machinery?***
Russell. Machinery did appeal to me but being brought up on a farm I was expected to do various farm jobs but I was never keen on

livestock; anything mechanical always appealed to me. In fact, when we had the firm of engineers, Jago from Plympton, to come up and do work on the traction engines in the early summer, before there was any threshing to do, I was always keen to be there.

Consequently when I left school I didn't go into farming. I went to work for Ernest Steer and Son at Kingsbridge, who were the Agricultural Engineers and Implement Makers. I worked in there for a few months but didn't like it. We were making Steer's balance ploughs, harrows and scarifiers, and blacksmithing. Everything was for horses and that is why I didn't like it so well. I stuck it for a while, it was interesting work and gave me a good knowledge of blacksmithing.

By then tractors were coming about and that was what I was interested in, working on that type of machinery and not horse stuff. After a few months I gave in my notice and the old man Steer didn't want me to leave and said "Where be 'ee gwain to git another job?"

Anyway on the Saturday morning I jumped on my bike and I rode down to Cantrell Works, between Bittiford and Ivybridge to a firm there called Watkins and Roseveare who were the agricultural engineers of a more modern type, they dealt with tractors. I went in and saw Mr. Watkins and told him I was looking for a job and I started on the Monday morning.

Reg. The firm started on a smallholding near Curtisknowle selling two wheeled tractors guided with handles!

Russell. They were Trusty tractors and that sort of thing, at Holsome Farm between Morleigh and Diptford. The two Watkins brothers, Ken and Ian were there before they moved down to Cantrell which were old sheds used for drying clay which was brought in from Redlake on Dartmoor. There was an under floor heating system to dry the clay, and a railway siding alongside. They took that over in about 1938.

It was during the war when I started there when tractors came across from America, imported on the Lend-lease scheme. They were in crates and had to be assembled, the majority were MM's and Olivers. They came down on the train to Ivybridge station and delivered up to Cantrell. We had to put on the spade lugs on the wheels and get them out to the farms.

Reg. We had a Standard Fordson at Woolston Farm from Watkins in 1942; we had been waiting twelve months for it.

Russell. I think they were £175 delivered to the farm.

Reg. Many farmers felt it would be too costly operating them, whereas horses fed off the farm but soon they realised that the tractors were ploughing ten acres a day compared with one acre with horses.

Russell. You didn't have to feed the tractor when it wasn't doing anything. You could just get off and leave it.

In the early days I went to work on a pushbike but when I was 16 I had a motorbike. I think the first one I had I pushed it more than I rode it! But after that I had a more reliable one.

Reg. Were you learning new techniques at Watkins?

Russell. I was taken on as a properly indentured apprentice and the pay was five shillings a week that is 25p in today's money. For that you were supposed to learn the trade of an agricultural engineer. Down there was a good base because during the war spares were not readily available and a lot of the parts had to be made and that was a good grounding for that trade. I was there for nearly five years.

They were importing American stuff mainly Olivers, M M's for which Watkins had an agency. Beare's of Newton Abbot dealt with Case and International. Later on we were able to get the first combine harvesters. They were hauled and powered driven by a tractor, of course the early tractors didn't have power drive but by 1947 the Fordson Major came in, fitted with power drive. Some combines were fitted with an engine but they were cumbersome and too wide for down here, you had to take the cutter bars and headers off to get them around.

The first ones came in crates and it took us a couple of weeks to put one together but after we had done a few we could do it in three days. Then self-propelled Massey Harris came in and I was sent up to Kilmarnock on a course, that was the 726 Bagger combine. A man had to ride on it collecting the corn in two hundredweight West of England sacks and sliding them down a shute on the ground.

Reg. *I remember picking them all up again.*

Russell. It wasn't long before they were fitted with tanks, which discharged into a trailer. I finished there in 1948 and within a week I had my call-up papers to do my National Service. While I was an apprentice I had a deferment but as soon as I finished I had one week's full pay £3. 10 shillings.

By that time I had met a local land girl that I took a shine to and we were married later on that year when I was in the RAF. I then had a married man's allowance which was eleven shillings a week, or was it eleven shillings a day, I can't remember but I thought that couldn't be bad.

Reg. *With your skills you must have gone into engineering?*

Russell. After our basic training I was called before a Board to decide what they were going to do with me and I said I had served an apprenticeship in agricultural engineering and I was asked if I would like to take a trade test to which I agreed. I went to Chigwell in Essex for three or four days to take the test, which I passed. I was posted then to big workshops between Cheshire and Flintshire and from then on it was a regular days work rebuilding vehicles mainly, I was in the engine shop most of the time.

We rebuilt engines up from scratch and completely reconditioned them, boxed them up and put them away for spares. They were from

Below: California Cross Filling Station and workshop. 1963

little Austin Tens to utility pickup trucks, right up to Perkins S6 marine engines for fitting in motor torpedo boats. There were also some big Thornycroft engines that went in the Cole's Cranes, ten or twelve litre engines.

I was there until early 1950 when I was demobbed by which time we had a young daughter and I had to find somewhere to live. My Grandfather used to live in Heathfield Cottage, near California Cross when he retired. It was an old cottage divided into two and we were able to take one half, which was one room down and one room up.

When I came out Ken Watkins wanted me to come back and work at Cantrell, but I wanted time to look around. A country boy being away doing National Service for two years had broadened my outlook considerably and I though I would job around, helping out, looking for an opportunity, which did arise within a short time.

I heard the old blacksmith's shop at California Cross, where old Fred Fox had been for years, was up for sale. I managed to find out the name of the owner who lived in Torquay and saw him and he said it was for sale. To cut a long story short I bought it with the six-acre field behind. I had only a year to raise the money but we got together enough money to buy it and after it was paid for and all the legal expenses settled we had £25 left to start on.

Reg. *The purpose was not to continue shoeing horses like Freddie Fox!*

Russell. The first job was to repair half the roof. I fortunately had an Uncle who did building work and he didn't want paying tomorrow so that was a fine start. When the roof was fixed I started repairing tractors, there was loads of work, too much very often.

We lived in Heathfield cottage until about 1955 when the Council built four new houses and we got the tenancy of one of them and moved there. There was no electricity but we did have water on tap and a Rayburn stove which gave us hot and cold water, t'was really good.

In 1956 I thought California Cross was a prime position for a petrol pump so I applied for permission. At that time there was some crisis going on at Suez. I tried again in 1957 and was fortunate in getting permission to put in the petrol pumps. We then became a petrol filling station as well as an agriculture engineer. We sold Esso petrol and I had two men, full time and one part time.

As time went on Jean and I were working extremely long hours, seven in the morning until ten at night, seven days a week and it got a bit much for us. In 1963 I began to take stock and thought why am I working like this, it was not a very good quality of life. We earned good money but we only had one daughter and there was no likelihood of any family taking it on.

One day the Esso Petroleum representative came to see me and I wasn't in a particularly good mood and I said, "If you could get somebody I would sell this place tomorrow." He said, "You've got a little gold mine here." and within a month he turned up with a man who had been kicked out of some part of Africa; he was an agricultural engineer and he bought it.

Reg. **But you didn't retire then, how old were you then?**

Russell. That was in 1963, I would have been 34 or 35 years old.

Reg. *You were right in your prime.*

Russell. I wanted to get away from the pressure of the work. It was difficult to get qualified staff and I was doing it all myself, that's no way of living. I thought 'what am I going to do now?'

I bought a large caravan and put it in a field of a farmer friend of ours for a couple of months while I was helping the new owner of the garage. I used to go there everyday, introducing him to various reps. and customers and then I began to look for something else.

I went out to Bigbury on my Uncle Alan's farm helping to save hay, and where he lived there were three derelict cottages, covered in brambles and I thought there is a possibility here to do something with them. I made an offer for them and bought them and we ended up with three building sites.

We moved our caravan out there and started work clearing the site and had a Woolaway bungalow erected where we lived, while we concentrated on developing the best site. We

built a nice bungalow and landscaped the site; we moved in and let the first one while we started on the third site. Someone came along who was very interested so we sold the site.

I enjoyed the building work and learned a lot, but I still wanted to get back into my old trade using my own tools again. I started looking around and came across a site in Loddiswell village, which appealed to me and was able to buy it from the owner. I always considered Loddiswell to be my parish; Bigbury was out one end, in and out the same road and was choc-a-bloc with traffic in the summer, I never really settled there.

We built our bungalow, Hazeltor in 1966/67 and having got somewhere to live I had to find a workshop. Down towards the bridge there was an old disused quarry, Rake Quarry that I could rent from John Sluggett. He said if I could get planning permission for a building there he would let the site for £25 per year and when I no longer needed it leave the building behind. I agreed to that, built a workshop and intended to keep the business on a small scale, I didn't want to get into the same position I was at California. All I needed was a small band of customers so I took on an apprentice, he was keen, a good lad, Andrew Lethbridge, and when he left he went on to College. I continued on my own for several years doing quite a lot of steel fabrication as well as tractors.

After a while a young fellow, Kevin Pidwell, came to me looking for a job and I took him on.

Below: Loddiswell Church gates made by Russell in 1977 for the Queen's Silver Jubilee.

He had learnt his trade with Sopers of East Allington, an excellent firm of engineers. We worked together for several years and he was a first class fellow, we always got on well together. He eventually took on more of the tractor work, which was getting more and more technical and some of it was beyond me so I was glad to leave it to him.

In the early 1980s I took Kevin in as a partner in the business; we extended the workshop and took on another man. I kept to the steel work and Kevin and Bill did the tractor work. I got courses for him up at John Deere's school in Nottingham; he was very keen and right up with these modern tractors, which left me behind.

When I retired in 1997 Kevin, who had married the daughter at Rake Farm, developed a workshop there in a covered yard with plenty of room for expansion. I had an auction of all my old equipment and junk, and 'cau, didn't it sell!' We had a tremendous sale. I was able to buy the workshop at the Quarry when Rake Farm was sold, which I have since sold.

Reg. Of more recent years you have developed your interest in motorbikes!

Russell. Yes, when we were married we had a motorbike and sidecar and I have always had one since I was 16. I have bought a few old bikes and restored them. I have been going to shows and rallies and won a lot of prizes with my best ones. I have now got two, which I will hang on to; one is a 1924 Norton, which I bought as a heap of scrap in South Wales and restored. My other one, the best one, is a 1947 Norton. Jean and I go away in the summer with the motorbike and sidecar and camp. Last year we went to France, right down to Bordeaux.

This year we are hoping to go to Norway, Sweden, across the new bridge to Denmark and right down into France. A few years ago we did the round trip up to John O'Groats and down to Land's End to raise money for Devon Air Ambulance. The weather up north wasn't very good, my golly, it rained up there! Several years ago we started a vintage display of motorbikes at Loddiswell Show and this has encouraged many others to renovate and show vintage bikes.

Above: The treasured Norton motorbike and sidecar. "When we were married we had a motorbike and sidecar and I have always had one since I was 16. "I have bought a few old bikes and restored them. I have been going to shows and rallies and won a lot of prizes with my best ones."
Below: Russell, President of Loddiswell Show 1993, presenting a cup to Dennis Sharland.

Gordon and Janet Beckley

Reg. This morning I've come to Witheridge, which is just on the west side of the Chapel Yard overlooking the Avon valley towards Rake. I have come to talk to Janet and Gordon Beckley. Janet., We were talking just now about how long you have been here.

Janet. We were married in 1958 and we went to Bideford for five years. In 1963 we came down to Loddiswell for Christmas and because of the snow we could not get back for three weeks. During that time Gordon was offered a job with Avon Farmers so we decided to stay. Ian was three; we stayed with Mum and Dad at Park View, as it was called then. Sheila and Owen had a flat converted over the baker's shop so we went and lived there for two years.

Lisa was born in 1965. At that time the land here was for sale so my Father purchased it. Hilary and Bill Field had this bungalow built and we had Lyndhurst, the one nearest the Village Cross road. When Hilary and Bill went to Salcombe to live, Mum and Dad came up from Park View to live here.

Dad died in 1981 and Mum stayed here on her

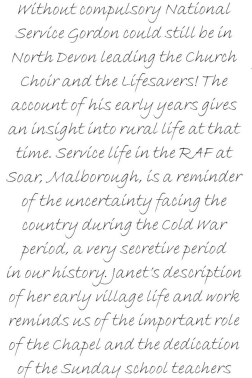

Without compulsory National Service Gordon could still be in North Devon leading the Church Choir and the Lifesavers! The account of his early years gives an insight into rural life at that time. Service life in the RAF at Soar, Malborough, is a reminder of the uncertainty facing the country during the Cold War period, a very secretive period in our history. Janet's description of her early village life and work reminds us of the important role of the Chapel and the dedication of the Sunday school teachers of that era.

own for a while but after Ian died in 1983 Mum was getting more frail so after a year or two we moved in here and sold Lyndhurst. Lisa was married to Andrew in September 1989 but, sadly, Mum had died in March of that year. We have lived here since 1987 and I think that's where we will stay.

Reg. Your young days were spent down at the Courtledge

Janet. Yes. In the house now called Lydia Cottage. I remember the pump and trough in the Courtledge and vaguely remember the beginning of the war in 1939, I was only two then.

Miss Michell used to bring her class of schoolchildren through the Courtledge to the Church Hall and I remember standing outside by the wall and saying I would like to go with them. So in the end Miss Michell took pity on me and said,

"Oh, come on then," so I tagged on with the rest, I was three and a half years old. Tony Hyne was about 18 months older than me, he was quite a slight, slender little chap and I was quite porky. Miss Michell used to laugh because he used to get behind me to push my chair in. Once she gave me a slap on my leg for giving my bottle of milk to someone else, I hated milk. If you went home and told your parents you had a smack or were reprimanded; they would say, "You must have deserved it."

On Sundays we went to Chapel three times, Service in the morning, Sunday School in the afternoon when up to thirty children attended and another Service in the evening. When I go to Church now or anywhere hand-bell ringing I know all the words of the hymns.

The highlight of the year at the Chapel was the Anniversary when we all had new frocks and hats. My Mum used to make all my clothes, she was very skilled. Again the Easter Bazaar was a great occasion. Of course there was no television then, life was much more sociable then. I can remember both Mother and Mr Scobell singing at concerts in the Hall. Leonard Scobell would sing a humorous song often about apple dumplings! Sometimes we would have our party down at Chevithorne with Margary and Sid Scoble and Mr. Ruby Tapp.

Schoolwork was always exhibited at Loddiswell Show; we used to make garments by sewing and knitting. Miss Common was a great embroiderer and Miss Michell was very keen on drama, not only at the School but produced plays for us to take part in, Red Earth, Peacemakers and the yearly pantomime.

Reg. What was your job during your working life?

Janet. When I left school in 1954 I went to Plymouth Technical College and did a year's business studies, shorthand and typing. When I finished there I went to work at Lloyds Bank, back in the days when everything was done by hand on ledgers and added up in your head. Mr MacMaster was the Manager then. I worked in there for four years 'till I got married in 1958 and then we went to Bideford to live. I was able to get a part time job in a solicitor's office, typing wills and all that sort of thing, not very interesting work.

Ian was born in 1960 that brings us up to 1963 when we came down here. When the children were small I helped Sheila in the shop and later when Ian died I worked for Roger Trembath at Quay Garage and later at Upper Union Road in the office. I was there for eleven years until I retired in 1997.

Reg. You were one of the teams of handbell ringers

Janet. Yes I have played for 25 or 30 years; Ann Carpenter was a little girl when we started. When we began we had enough players for four teams, a lot of people gradually dropped out, as they didn't find it was their scene and the practices took up too much time. I remember Mrs Eckett and Mrs Hallmark started with us but eventually we were left with about eight which included Angela Freeman, Muriel Carpenter, Sylvia Hallam, Sylvia Walke, Ruth Hyne, Hazel Lethbridge and myself. We were later joined by Sally Dutton, Catherine Taylor and Eileen Gray. My daughter Lisa and Ann Carpenter rang with us as teenagers but as some of our members have moved away we have formed a new team which includes some younger ringers.

In the past we have competed in competitions and taken part in a number of rallies in different parts of the country, sometimes we mass ring with other groups having practised set pieces separately. We then play together under a conductor, it is good fun. We have been as far afield as Sheffield, London and several other places for workshops where we learn different methods of ringing. Some ring four in hand, others off the table. We have our own rally in the Village Hall each year when we invite other teams to join us, like Harmony Four Hundred, who are mainly musicians based at Newton Abbot, they have about 300 bells so you know what a big team they are.

Reg. Gordon, I understand you came from North Devon!

Gordon. Yes, a little place called Ford about five miles from Bideford. It was more of a hamlet than a village, the water supply was from wells, we were fortunate as ours was at the bottom of the garden. My grandparents who lived further up the hill were not so fortunate and my brother and I had to go a quarter of a mile up a lane with two buckets to fetch their water. It was marvellous how the wells were built, always round and very nicely built with stone.

My Father worked on the land and Mother worked at the Rectory, the old rectory at Alwington, near Woodtown. When we started school about six of us from the hamlet had to walk about two and a half miles. We set off mornings, hand in hand, up a winding lane meandering around the fields until we eventually came to the church. The school was right beside it in Alwington and I was there until I was eleven years old when I went on to Bideford School. I remember when my Father worked on the farm; Mother would cut a hunk of bread, a lump of cheese and a cold bottle of tea. Some mornings when it was pouring with rain he wore a big sack around his waist and a sack around his shoulders, gaiters on his legs and hob-nailed boots. He would lean up against the hedge to have his lunch and then carry on working.

Reg. Farm workers often wore West of England sacks to keep themselves dry in wet weather.

Gordon. My Father had to give up working on the land and my family moved to a place near Westward Ho! My Mother made me go to Church three times on Sundays until I was 17, just like Janet. In the summer we had services on the Front at Westward Ho! I was a choirboy and used to carry the Cross and all the congregation would follow down to the Front with the Vicar and all the visitors following. They gathered around to sing hymns and at Christmas we would all go down and sing carols. After I had been going to the Church for a while I helped

Right: National Service at RAF Hope Cove. 1955 "...I was 21 when I joined the Forces in 1954. I did my 'square bashing' at Wilmslow...,"

with Communion as a Server. The Vicar asked me to pass the bread around. At morning and evening services I carried the Cross followed by the boys who sat in the choir pews. My Mother made me do that until I was nearly 18. When you get about 17 you start to branch out and become more self-conscious. In those days you always did what your parents told you without question.

I joined a gang of lads when I was 18 to act as Lifesavers down at Westward Ho beach. We were swimming nearly all the year round and we obtained our Lifesaving Certificates. Our job was to patrol the beach and make sure people didn't go out too far, we had a life belt ready on the slipway. One of my old friends went on to become a very professional lifesaver. He now has an amusement arcade at Westward Ho and I always visit him when I go up there. I was always fond of playing tennis and table tennis, and of course swimming.

I started my apprenticeship as a carpenter at Bideford and continued until I was 21 when I joined the Forces in 1954. I did my 'square bashing' at Wilmslow, as I did not want to go to RAF Chivenor, which was right on my doorstep. It was a very working aerodrome then and being 21 I tried to avoid too much work. I was then asked where I would like to be stationed and I said, "South Devon" so they put me down at RAF Hope Cove. It was a small camp and I spent two years there as a tele-printer operator. I did a course up in Chippenham near Devises for 15 weeks, type writing and tele-printing, then I was

Below: Staff of Kingsbridge branch of Lloyds Bank with Janet seated in front row. 1956

posted back to RAF Hope Cove, which was based in Malborough.

The runway at Soar had been removed by then and they built a great concrete bunker which was half underground. This was at the time of the Cold War with Russia, when there was a fear of nuclear attack. It was one of 17 emergency regional headquarters in the country and would have provided accommodation for up to 150 Government officials in the event of a nuclear war. It was on the site of the old camp, some of the huts were still there but a new camp had then been built back in Malborough. We travelled to and fro by armoured lorry to the bunker.

At that time there was night flying around the country, which was monitored there. The squadron used to go to the bunker to direct the aircraft and I always remember a colleague of mine made a mistake on directing a pilot out over the sea, he directed him too low and he ditched. Fortunately he survived and sometime later he came to the bunker and made himself known especially to my friend who had ditched him. He had been very worried about this and was very relieved to see him back and we had a bit of a 'do' in the Sergeant's Mess. The pilot joked, "You tried to get rid of me, but I've come back."

Some nights when I was at Hope Cove I would

Below: With the building section of Avon Farmers Ltd 1964 "I was with Avon Farmers Builders for many years until many of the Farm Improvements Schemes were completed."

go up and help send messages; as it was a small camp sometimes it was only half a dozen messages. I would ask the Commanding Officer if I could borrow a bike to ride back to camp after midnight to which he agreed. One night I was coming down and had a serious accident with transport coming up the lane, I saw the headlights coming and the next thing I knew I was in sick quarters.

In the bunker I had an office on my own with two teleprinters, one outgoing and one incoming. My job was sending and receiving messages, which I reported to the Sergeant whose office was straight across from mine. Our offices were on the top floor and down the stairs was the operations room in the basement where a massive circular map covering the whole of the South West peninsular. They used to direct the aircraft by radar, giving them their height and direction. Their positions were monitored by our lads around the large map table, it was on a massive scale and they used to push long rods to plot the positions of aircraft as they changed course.

The camouflaged bunker was a massive building and was built as a Command Unit for the South West and to provide accommodation for an administration unit in case of nuclear attack. It was guarded at night by dog patrols and when I was late cycling back I had to ring the gate keeper to make sure the dogs were under control because after a certain time the dogs were let loose all night long within the perimeter fence.

Reg. How many staff worked there?

Gordon. I think there were about 15 civilians. One of the civilians, Jack Bolton, still lives in Kingsbridge, he was a mechanical and electrical engineer, who lived in Kingsbridge but spent most of his working time at the bunker. The Squadron was about 200 to 250 RAF personnel who lived at their barracks in Malborough, later developed into Cumber Close. The houses were built for the Officers and NCOs and were later taken over by the Council. I was there from 1955 to 1957 and when I was demobbed the camp was closed soon afterwards.

Reg. The Nissan huts were sold by auction and

we dismantled two of them and re-erected them at Lilwell.

Gordon. We used to have dances at the camp and a lot of dances at the Town Hall in Kingsbridge and that's where I met Janet. When I was demobbed I went with Scobles, the Builders in Wallingford Road for a while and in 1963 the site was taken over by Avon Farmers Ltd., a buying and selling group that also had a building section. I was responsible for the carpentry side and used to go out on to the farms with a colleague called Bill Scuse, doing work under the Farm Improvement Scheme. The Building section grew employing 25 staff under their Manager David Cobham and later Dennis Thorne.

I was with Avon Farmers Builders for many years until many of the Farm Improvements Schemes were completed. We had been building new milking parlours, silage pits and grain stores and a limited number of domestic house improvements and extensions. The last job I did was at Tacket Wood; I was overseer of a building conversion there. The group then split up and many of the staff started their own businesses.

Reg. **What did you do then?**

Gordon. I heard they wanted a maintenance man down at the Salcombe Hotel; I got a job there and was there about eleven years. In the winter I was doing maintenance and was able to bring in Loddiswell builders to help. Often in the summer months I worked on the ferryboat taking visitors from the hotel across to the Portlemouth side.

I then took the post of Caretaker at the Fosse Road Secondary School in Kingsbridge, which also entailed being around for evening classes. My back was beginning to give me some trouble as there were so many stairs and I was able to move to the Primary School in Belle Cross Road which was all on one level. Eventually my back and hips were troubling me and I had to take early retirement at the age of 60, that would have been in 1993.

Since my retirement I have continued to be involved in many village activities. When I was still in the RAF Bert Elliott was Secretary of Loddiswell Show and if you had two spare arms

or hands he would grab them and give you something to do. Janet and I put up the advertising posters around the area and ran the ice cream stall for many years.

I was in the Loddiswell Inn Euchre Team and also the Loddiswell tennis team for a long time. I really enjoyed being a member of the South Hams Table Tennis League in Kingsbridge and when I was in North Devon in 1954 I was successful in winning the 21st World Championship Club Competition run by the English Table Tennis Association.

I became interested in raising money for different causes and this led to the Friday night bingos in the Village Hall when I agreed to become the bingo caller. Ian Lethbridge has helped me in recent years, and my services have been required in other villages. One of the causes we supported was in aid of Muscular Dystrophy, a muscular disease from which our son Ian had died at the age of 23 years in 1983. We helped towards the Kingsbridge and District Branch of M.D. who raised over £60,000 in 15 years.

Below: Table tennis championship with John Barry 1968 "...I really enjoyed being a member of the South Hams Table Tennis League ...in 1954 I was successful in winning the 21st World Championship Club Competition.

Beryl Brooking

Reg. I am visiting Beryl who lives at No 2 Little Gate, Loddiswell, which overlooks the Great Gate valley, and Station Road on the other side. Now I'm not sure if your parents have always lived in Loddiswell?

Beryl. I think my Grandfather ran away from home to North Devon, his parents were farmers but he went and learnt shoe making. My Grandma was Cornish, she was a very ladylike woman, but was the delicate one of the family and they lived at London Apprentice, near St. Austell.

She moved when another woman arrived in the kitchen, things did not always go right at home and she moved out and went to the Vicar of Ashprington, near Totnes as a help to the Vicar's wife, they were all do-gooders in those days, things for the poor and all that. Grandma was in her element doing that, she was a wonderful seamstress and she met Grandad there, one was as rough as the other was ladylike. Being delicate she had six children in eight years!

They moved to Stoke fleming then. My father was born at Stoke Fleming where he worked with his father and brother making, repairing and selling boots and shoes. He and his brother

Beryl's optimistic and enthusiastic approach to life was supportive to her husband Glyn. Beryl was born in Loddiswell, attended the local school before moving to boarding school and a job in London. Her husband's pleasing personality was soon recognised and he was quickly promoted to a managerial role, which enabled them to live very full lives. On Glyn's death Beryl returned to live in Loddiswell.

went into the Great War but his brother was injured, and was on an 100 per cent Disability Pension. There wasn't a living for all three of them there so Dad came to Loddiswell in the early 1920s and lodged with Mrs Timewell, at Prospect House. He bought some old cottages on the Bank, knocked them down and built two brick houses there, numbers 1 and 2 The Bank, Loddiswell, and moved into No. 1 when he married Laura Luscombe in 1925. It was built with a shoemaker's shop for repairing boots and shoes, but new ones were commercially made by then. Your father, Reg, bought number two.

I was born in 1926 and when I was five years old I went to Loddiswell School. We were not separated from the boys as they were in some town schools. We used to play hopscotch and go for walks with our hoops. In those days you could go for walks without your parents, down to the river without any fear. There was not so much communication in those days so we didn't know what happened elsewhere. I remember walking to Bantham and back, and when I was older we used to cycle with a crowd to play on the beach. My sister Muriel was born in 1933.

Above: Beryl and Muriel with their parents, Bert and Laura Bowden. 1946

Reg. **Who was the teacher when you began at Loddiswell School?**

Beryl. There was a Miss Whittle who took the infants, I think the head teacher was Mrs Foot but she was away sick for some time and Mr Higman came as a supply teacher. Miss Margaret Common came in my last year. I then won a scholarship to Totnes School and was there as a boarder. It was Totnes or Crediton, I wished afterwards I had gone to Crediton, I think I would have studied more there. Totnes was very good, but then the war came in the middle of it when I was thirteen. The school was disrupted and we were unable to study maths, which was my best subject, University was out of the question.

I left school at sixteen and a half and went to London in September 1942 and got a job in the Civil Service, Inland Revenue, first of all in the Collector of Taxes Dept in Grosvenor Street. Then I moved to the Inspector of Taxes, just around the corner, in North Audley Street, it was near the Grosvenor area and the American Embassy. I meet Glyn up there, not in Loddiswell where he lived.

Reg. **What was he doing up in London?**

Beryl. Glyn was taking his pilot's course at St John's Wood at that time. He used to come down to Loddiswell on leave to see his Grandma, and my Father used to keep in touch with all who came in the shop so he knew who was where. Father said one day, "Oh, Beryl's living at Harrow at the moment with an Aunt until she gets her accommodation sorted out." Glyn came to see us, he didn't take much notice of me, I was just a schoolgirl, he really came to Auntie's for a meal. I moved into London and didn't keep in touch but eventually he called to see me, so it went on from there. In 1946 I was transferred back to Newton Abbot and we got married in 1947.

Reg. I remember Glyn at school before he went with Northcott's down at the Concrete Works, near Loddiswell Bridge. There was a little office there checking lorries in and out with concrete blocks and goods!

Beryl. He was the tea boy! No, what really happened, he had gone into Balkwills, the Coal Merchant to train in bookkeeping, and one day Bob Northcott met Glyn, who was riding his bicycle, and said, "I would like you to come and work for me." Glyn said, "I can't do that as mother has signed me on a Contract." Anyway it was sorted out and he went to work for Northcotts. He didn't look back because he always seemed to be in the right place at the right time.

At the beginning of the war, before he was old enough to join up, he went to work in Northcott's Civil Engineering Dept. that was building the Royal Marine's barracks at Lympstone. He gained experience in different sides of the business before he volunteered for the Air Force. He came out in 1946 and came back to the Exeter office; there were a lot of men coming out about then so they found a place for him at the limestone quarry at Berry Head.

We bought the Preston's shop and cottage in Loddiswell in 1947 and during the time we were there we took on the Post Office work. We had been married a couple of years and our daughter Denise was born in 1949.

They were re-opening a quarry down at Landrake and Glyn was sent down to see what

Above: Glyn presenting a bouquet to Mrs Northcott at Greystone Quarry dinner, Launceston, 1957. Beryl is seated at the table.

he could make of it; that turned out OK. We were at the Post Office for eight years to 1955 and then we went to Saltash for 14 years. They had a big quarry at Launceston, just over the border into Cornwall, that was Greystone Quarry. It proved to be the best quarry of the group, Glyn started that up from scratch, it was originally a Cornwall County Quarry but hadn't done any thing for years.

Then Northcotts amalgamated with FJ Moore, Mills of Stoneycombe and Bents of Taunton. They were family businesses, and Bob Northcott, who was not much older than Glyn, became the Managing Director. Bob had taken over from his Father.

Bob approached (English China Clay) ECC and together they took them over and formed ECC Quarries, which is now a French firm.

The arrangement was that Horace Bailey, Glyn and Arthur Peace, who had trained with the company, were made directors of the company. Horace Bailey's Father was a signalman at Kingsbridge Station; Arthur Peace's brother worked in the Gazette Office. They were made

directors, Arthur was responsible for sales, Glyn was mainly with production, mining and working with the Unions, Horace was the PR man really, he like the entertainment side.

It was quite a big concern and then ECC Quarries took over a big company in Henley-on-Thames called Sidney Green, a Civil Engineering Company that built motorways and whatnot. The Company was eventually run down and they formed Amalgamated Asphalt, which is now Bardens. Croft Granite Company in Leicester, and Body Engineering Company in Carnforth and Sheffield, then joined the Group.

Reg. **Where were you living during this time?**

Beryl. We were a year in Leicester before we had a house built in Henley-on-Thames. It cost us £16,000 and it has since been sold for £525,000 and they have also sold off a piece of ground to build another house.

The Company had a big quarry in Leicester employing about 800 men in six or seven different Unions. They had to cut that down because they were top heavy and Glyn used to go up from Henley to sort it out, sometimes he would stay a night.

Glyn was born in 1922 and when he was 56 years old, that would have been in 1978, he had a heart operation and had to slow down a bit. He was up and about in two weeks but wasn't supposed to work. His Secretary used to come down to do the office work. He was driving a car again in six weeks but he was never quite the same. It was early days of the aorta operations and he had bypasses done at the same time. He showed no symptoms whatsoever, just some breathlessness and some pain at night. By then there was a new Managing Director who was re-organising things and he wanted us to move down to Exeter. We didn't know how the family would feel about this as they lived only two miles away from us. We moved down to Shaldon and Glyn took early retirement, he wasn't all that fit.

I never liked it there, we were the wrong age when we went there; if we had gone there younger it would have been different. Glyn became involved in various things, he was a prison visitor and he also represented the public

Above: Bert Bowden at the door of his shoe shop in Fore Street. 1924-1963

on the Department of Health and Social Services (DHSS) tribunals at Exeter, Torquay and Plymouth and that kept him occupied. He was failing in health as he had cancer for years. By the time he knew he had it, it was too late to do anything. Glyn died in April 1991.

Reg. You felt a bit isolated at Shaldon!

Beryl. Yes, I did, I told Glyn before he died that if he went before me I would put the house on the market and move back to Loddiswell. He said, "You must do as you wish," and I did. I sold it in 1991 and by October or November I came here to Little Gate.

The house at Shaldon was valued the previous year at £60,000 more than I sold it for as the prices had slumped. Some people from Italy saw the property and wanted to move in within three weeks.

Reg. Buying and selling is balanced, you sell at a lower price but you are also able to buy at a lower price. Now what do you do besides looking after your beautiful garden?

Beryl. I raise a lot of plants from seed, but not as much as I did, and I help my daughter Denise and her husband Peter, who now live in Newton Abbot so I see quite a lot of them.

My daughter has had problems with her health in the last few years.

Reg. Can we go back to your Dad's days when he worked in the shop? I used to visit him on school days as so many other people did, everyone knew him as Bert Bowden. He was always busy mending shoes or putting hobnails in boots.

Beryl. and whistling all the time!

Reg. When the War came he was made Air Raid Warden. Do you remember that?

Beryl. I was only home at weekends and I knew they had evacuees, in fact one of them is living in Newton Abbot now, Joan Kelly, that was the first lot that came from the Elephant and Castle, there were two girls, Joan and Lily.

The first day she was there she let someone's tyres down, she was only about four year old. Of course I wouldn't know how to do it, but she did. They went home when the bombing subsided but later when the doodlebugs started then Ruth and another Jewish girl came. (Ruth of course, later married Ken Hyne)

My Grandfather lived with us as well, that is my Mother's Father, Tom Luscombe. He was a brother of Garland Luscombe who lived at Churchstow, he was the eldest and the eldest was always called Garland. His daughter was Valerie Luscombe and coincidently she married Ron Garland.

I remember being at home when Plymouth was bombed and going up to Village Cross where we could see the oil storage tanks blazing. Of course I was away most of the time, I went to London in 1942. We were in the middle of the London bombing and I was living in Baker Street then. It was mostly doodlebugs then, the V1's. You could hear them coming as they would hum and when it stopped you had to quickly get under cover before they dropped. If you could hear them you knew they were near. When you are young you don't worry about things like that.

I remember VE Day; the day after was a public holiday and we went to Buckingham Palace. There was a girl called Dorothy Pedrick from Kingsbridge who was living where I was and we went together. We were outside Buckingham Palace and someone tapped me on the shoulder, it was Desmond Hill's Mother who was staying at Croydon and she said, "What are you doing here?" It was funny, both coming from Loddiswell and celebrating the victory in Europe outside Buckingham Palace.

We were at the Loddiswell Post Office at the time of the Queen's Coronation and I was back again for the Queen's Golden Jubilee in 2002.

Winnie Jeffery

Reg. I have come to talk to Winnie Jeffery in her new flat in Ashwood Park. You have only recently moved here, Winnie?

Winnie. I have been here since the end of November 2001. I was down with Maureen and Peter from the end of January until November. Before I came here I lived at Sunnyside for 64 years.

*Reg. **When did you come to Loddiswell?***

Winnie. I came on the 11th November 1937.

I came to live with my Aunt, old Mrs Butters, who needed company and help after her husband died. My sister came over first but she didn't like it so I came and I worked for the Winzers at Great Gate. When they left I worked for Mrs Scobell at Reveton Farm for a while and then for Miss Pearce at Cross House as a housekeeper.

*Reg. **I remember old Mr. Butters had a pony and trap.***

Winnie. He kept the pony in a shed at the top of the garden, which was very big and stretched right up to the Chapel Yard wall. It was a market garden at one time where Alf Hine grew vegetables when he lived in Sunnyside. He was the Father of Bill, Walter and

Winnie epitomises our image of the ideal Granny. Her helpful and kindly nature has endeared her both to family and village community. Years of working in their shop gave her close contact with the village. Her husband, Sydney was always fascinated by the mechanism of clocks and he became very skilled in repairing them. They both contributed and supported the Congregational Church over a long period of time. Syd was Superintendent of the Sunday school, Secretary and then Treasurer.

Ethel Hine and later the family moved to Hazelwood.

Reg. Sydney, I believe, lived at Sorley Cottage with his parents until he was three years old and then the family moved to Virginia Cottage, here in Loddiswell. He was well known for his skills in repairing bicycles and clocks.

Winnie. Yes, he used to work there. I got to know him soon after I came. We went together for about five years, the place was full of clocks which he studied as they fascinated him. I could show you a book of all his clocks, even the Church clock that he repaired. He took the church clock to pieces and brought them home to repair them. The weights were so heavy they went through his new workshop floor. Anyway, Edmond Diamond quickly came and renewed it, it was a laugh! I've even got the bill for the work he did. It was in September 1962 and cost £60

*Reg. **What was your impression of Loddiswell?***

Winnie. It was very nice but it was very dark and I was afraid, as I had been used to street lighting. I had come from Porth in the Rhondda valley. I was born at Pontypridd and Porth was

Above: Sydney in his workshop "...clocks... they fascinated him. ...he took the church clocks to pieces and brought them home to repair them. The weights were so heavy they went through his new workshop floor!"

the next village up the valley. It was a mining area, my father was a miner. He died aged 48 from silicosis.

When the war came, Sydney did not pass his medical for the army, they said he would have to go to a chronometer factory so he sold up everything and he wasn't called from that day to this so he had to start all over again.

During the war years Syd spent a while in Lockyer Street Hospital during the time when Plymouth was being bombed. Everyone had to be carried down to the basement shelters during the raids, it was very distressing.

Syd was later in the Home Guard Signals Section and he was on duty with Leslie Adams when the group photograph was taken, so they, and also Wally Tarr, were not in it. Lionel Ryder was the sergeant in the Home Guard then.

We were married in 1942 and bought Sunnyside in 1944 from Mr Richard Willing. (S R Willing)

Reg. When you came to Sunnyside, the building underneath was still a linhay?

Winnie. It was four stables with big black, tarred doors in front. I believe they were used for changing horses on the route to Wrangaton in the days of the stagecoaches. We altered those of course. In the meantime Syd had a bedroom at Sunnyside and a workshop upstairs to do his clocks.

We altered the stables; Powleslands had the end

store to keep their fuel, coke and all that, for the London House Stores Bakery and Mr. Johnny Marsh, Senior had the next one to keep his car in, Nurse Ramsey had the next one and we kept one for a wash-house cum-store. The standpipe and the toilet were out in the garden. Syd and Mr. Griffith brought the water indoors after we went there. Mr. Griffith was at the Turk's Head Inn.

Eventually we converted the end two stores on the ground floor into a workshop and later the other two, we had a big window put in and made a shop. We did very well there. Later we built a workshop and garage at the back: which we sold in 1988 to Geraint Ball who used it as a tool shop. After five years he sold it to Ken Ball and he built a house where the filling station used to be.

Reg. Both you and Sydney were very involved with the Congregational Church?

Winnie. Sydney took a very active role there; he was Superintendent of the Sunday school, and was Secretary first and then Treasurer. Then he became Manager of the Church, he was very conscientious with his church work and I supported and helped him. We had a Women's Guild that was very active and still is. They used to call it the Cradle Roll.

Reg. What do you remember of the war years?

Winnie. I remember the Forces going through with their tanks, knocking down one of the houses at Fowlescombe. I knew the person who lived there, Lewis Luscombe. A 28-ton American tank slipped off the transporter as it rounded the bend. It knocked down half the house as Lewis was having his tea in the kitchen and his wife was upstairs putting the children to bed. Fortunately they were not injured. The Americans used the Congregational Hall and Great Gate cottage. I was working then for Miss Pearce at Cross House then and I remember that one of them was hurt and Nurse Guest went down to see him.

At this time there was rationing and Mr Burgess at the Post Office, Bert Elliott and many others kept asking Sydney if he would install and sell Pool petrol which was the standard petrol in the wartime.

Above: David and Peter by the Pool Petrol Pump in 1952. "Mr Norman Rogers and Roger Dury had a race to see who would buy the first gallon and Mr Rogers was the first to buy it at one shilling and eleven pence a gallon, ..."

Below: Syd at the wheel of his Austin 7 at Loddiswell Show. 1986 "We loved that little car but we sold it in 1991; it went up to the Wye valley to a place called Whitchurch. We were sorry to see it go."

Reg. **When you installed the petrol pumps, who dug the pits for the tanks?**

Winnie. Tom Soper was one and Gerald Ryder, there were quite a few who helped with picks and shovels. Walter Hine drove the lorry that took the rubble down to Glebe, and Peter, who was small then remembers going with him. I can't remember but someone locally put the tanks in. Mr Norman Rogers and Roger Dury had a race to see who would buy the first gallon and Mr Rogers was the first to buy it at one shilling and eleven pence a gallon, that is just over two pence a litre in today's currency. The petrol was issued against coupons, which involved a lot of paper work, which I used to do. Most things were rationed and coupons were used for food and clothing.

The garden was too big for us so we eventually sold two plots, Richard Tucker bought one, and Dick and Blodwyn Bowen bought the top one near Village Cross road.

We retired from the shop in 1981 and it was let to a succession of tenants.

Sydney drove a little Austin 7, which we took to various shows including the Kingsbridge Vintage Show; we went to many other shows as well. We loved that little car but we sold it in 1991; it went up to the Wye valley to a place called Whitchurch. We were sorry to see it go but Syd could not look after it any longer.

Reg. **Can we talk a little about the family?**

Winnie. The eldest is David, he lives at Malborough but his health isn't too good.

Peter comes next, he lives next door with Maureen and they service holiday homes.

Then there is Paul who is a social worker at Tavistock, working with disabled adults. John is the youngest; he was a Headmaster at Norton-sub-Hamdon for ten years and then moved to Ilminster Primary School where there are 150 children.

Reg. **You are interested in photography!**

Winnie. Yes, I took a lot of photographs and so did Syd, I've got books of them. I also like doing crossword puzzles, knitting and crochet work, and in the past I have put a lot of entries in Loddiswell Show.

Dennis Hine

*R*eg. *Your early days were spent at Hown Farm, Dennis!*

Dennis. Yes, I lived there with my Grandfather, Grandmother, Mother and my Father, Jim Hine, and my two sisters, Ruby and Pearl. We kept about a dozen cows that we milked by hand, there weren't milking machines in those days, we used steel milking buckets. Calves were reared on to yearlings and store cattle and were sold in Kingsbridge Market. I started hand milking when I was about fourteen years old and sometimes had to milk a couple before I went to school. The farm was about 56 acres, it wasn't a big farm, and the work was done with horses, horse and cart or wain.

Reg. **Did you go to school from there?**

Dennis. I went to Loddiswell School; the teachers then were Miss Common, Miss Michell and Miss Todd. They were good teachers and I got on well there, I liked the lessons but was not very keen on sports. After that I went to Kingsbridge Secondary Modern School in Fosse Road. They played football and rugby on a field up near Century Farm; we had to walk up there. I played football but the main thing I enjoyed was

Dennis' account of his early life at Hown Farm brought back many happy memories for him. The farm overlooks the beautiful Avon Valley, the river and the small-disused primrose railway line. On the death of his Grandparents he had to leave Hown and take a job with the local quarry. He eventually took early retirement and worked as a gardener, a job he really loved. The family were always involved with the Congregational Church and Dennis has worked untiringly to support it.

gardening over Belle Cross Road where the Primary School is now, I used to love that. I looked forward to being at home on the farm at weekends, it was my country life.

I left school in 1952 when I was 15 and worked for my Grandfather on the farm. I did all sorts of jobs; there are so many jobs to do on the farm. Milking was seven days a week, and had to be done twice a day. It was put into churns and taken to our milk stand down at the Avon Mill to be collected by one of the Totnes lorries.

We grew about nine acres of hay and five or six acres of corn, a bit of oats, a bit of barley and some dredge corn, that is mixed corn. An acre of mangolds and a few turnips were fed to the cattle. Most of the work was done with horses, and some was done by a contractor. The root crops had to be scuffled with a three-row horse scuffle and then hoed out by hand. We grew a few potatoes to be self- supporting but I enjoyed it all.

You could tell the time by the trains on the Kingsbridge railway, passengers and goods. I have seen agricultural machines coming down to Kingsbridge for Mr Steer, cattle food for the different merchants, and, on Store Sale days, trucks loaded with cattle going up the line for Cornwall or the North Country. My half-day off was on Wednesdays and I would go into Kingsbridge Market, which was on Wednesdays in those days. Westcotts or Mr Shinner would be hauling coal from the Goods Yard with a horse and cart.

*Reg. **When did you leave Hown?***

Dennis. I worked at Hown about thirteen years until Grandfather died in 1966 and I then moved in with my Father who was living here at Sunnydene. I would like to have carried on farming but the Landlord, Mr Hetherington, wanted the farm and I had to look for some other work.

A job came up at the Quarry where my Father worked so I said I would try it, but during the first couple of years I didn't know whether to stay or leave. I was making concrete blocks at Torr, the concrete works at New Bridge had been closed and the business transferred to Torr.

My job was to go to the mixer plant and take a skip load of concrete in a dumper to the block machine, to and fro, every day. Jack Hack loaded the finished blocks on to the lorries with a forklift; previously he worked for Jack Baker on his threshing machine.

There were about 30 men at the quarry when I started, about 15 from Loddiswell, some from East Allington and Kingsbridge but as things became more mechanised numbers dropped to about 15 altogether. Four were then offered jobs driving lorries hauling stones from the quarry face up to the crusher plant, I thought I would enjoy that, a nice little job. Michael Hack drove the second lorry and we took the stones and tipped them into the crusher controlled by Dennis Sharland. When they were broken they went through a second crusher looked after by Fred Hine and on to three bins which sorted it out into two-inch and right down to dust.

Below: Dennis loading stone at Torr Quarry with a Ruston Bucyrus. 1972

Above: Working in the garden at Sunnydene 2002 " I've cut the grass on the village greens for many years and I also grow quite a lot of vegetables and a few flowers at Sunnydene."

Above: Discussing the entries at Loddiswell Show 1958. Left to Right Leonard Wood, Jim Hine (Dennis's Father) Harold Lethbridge and Dennis.

The stones at the quarry face were loaded by my Father who drove the Ruston Bucyrus, a tracked machine with steel cables to lift the jib and bucket.

The Manager of the quarry, when I started, was Mr Brooks from Plymouth, he was a proper chap, Mr Arthur Grant, who was a Director of the Company, had moved on to Exeter. Then the Works Foreman was Percy Johns and he was there when the quarry was closed down. I was there for fourteen years, the last four years I was driving the Ruston Bucyrus, and then, in about 1976, they moved me to New England Quarry, down between Lee Mill and Yealmpton. We had a company van to travel. Les Brimacombe and a few others from Torr and Kingsbridge, also went.

I was a navvy driver at the face of the quarry loading stone again, that was my job down there. Later they had a 'Bright' machine to load it. It worked by hydraulics with a two-ton bucket on the jib and that was a lovely machine to drive. The one problem was it was not self-propelled; it was on wheels and to move it around I had to drop the bucket into a lorry, which would push or pull me where I wanted to go. That quarry closed in 1995 and we were all made redundant. I was offered a job at Moorcroft near Plymouth and I asked if the job would be secure for the next five or six years. "No," they said, "it could be six months and you could be out again." I said, "That isn't much good to me," so I began to think what I wanted to do. I was always keen on gardening so I thought I will go out on my own and do work in people's gardens, grass cutting, tilling their vegetable gardens but mostly tidying flower beds, particularly for older people who can't cope with it. I've cut the grass on the village greens for many years and I also grow quite a lot of vegetables and a few flowers at Sunnydene.

Reg. **You have won a number of prizes at Loddiswell Show over the years!**

Dennis. Yes, I have done very well there, winning and as runner-up.

Reg. **You are closely associated with the Congregational Church!**

Dennis. During their lifetimes my Grandparents were active within the Congregational Church, Grandfather was Secretary for many years and I am still involved there. We have a little Church at Torcross as well so I go there on Sunday afternoons for the Service at 3 pm. I have done that for 32 years and I still help to keep it going.

Dennis and Doris Sharland

*R*eg. *I have come to No.4 New Road to see Dennis and Doris Sharland. Dennis, you have not always lived in Loddiswell?*

Dennis. No, I was born in Exeter, at a place called Farringdon in 1921. My Father worked on an estate there and then he moved down to Lord Falmouth's estate, at Tresillian, near Truro. We lived in one of the cottages there just above the church. I went to the local school there and later I went to Senior School at Probus, by bus in the mornings and in the evening we had to walk home which was about two and a half miles. My parents went to Church there and I had to go with them, I had to go even if they didn't. I was in the choir and belonged to the Sunday school. In the summer we had trips down the Fal to Falmouth on a paddle steamer. There were four of us children but only my brother Jim and I survived. My sister and younger brother died in infancy. When we left Tresillian we went to Newton Abbot and stayed with an Aunt for a while until Father got another job, which was at Dawlish

Before settling in Loddiswell Dennis experienced many homes. He was called up at the beginning of the Second World War and served in many war zones as a medical orderly. He was demobbed in 1946 and when his family moved to Loddiswell he was able to find employment leading to a job at Torr Quarry where he remained until his retirement. Doris was born in Well Street and is able to recall the early life of families living there in the early 20th century. Both have been very involved with the Church, Dennis as Secretary and Church Warden and Doris helped with the cleaning for many years.

working on the farm at Langdon Institute. We went on to Shaldon where I went to school until I was 14. Then I went to work for Mrs Bradshaw looking after her dogs and gardening and later for Mr Osborne in his green grocer's business. I then saw a job advertised at St. Martins in the Scilly Isles and went there working in the bulb fields. I was there for a couple of years and then to North Devon, working for a Mr. Howard at Beaford on the farm. When the war started I wanted to be nearer my parents who were then living in Exeter, so I moved back and started working in the gardens of the Princess Elizabeth Orthopaedic Hospital, near Topsham Barracks. I was there about two years and then I had my calling up papers on my 20th birthday and was sent to Dorchester. I was there for eight weeks basic army training and then transferred to the Signal Corps at Huddersfield. This did not suit me and I was transferred to the Medical Corps. I did my training at Leeds Hospital and then I was moved

to Edinburgh Castle as a Medical Orderly. I was then transferred for two years on the main island at Scapa, in the Orkneys, before returning to Edinburgh Castle and joined a Field Ambulance Unit, which was sent to Aberdeen. By this time the invasion had taken place and soon after D-Day we went across to Ostend in Belgium. We joined forces with a Canadian Division and moved with them through Holland to the borders of Germany. Troops were then wanted for South-East Asia and I was recalled to Aldershot where we regrouped and then sent out to East Africa to Mombassa.

I worked there in the Military Hospital as Wardmaster, mainly on night duty. I was responsible for the bed allocation, which I reported to the Head Office, so they could decide how many cases they could send to the hospital.

We regrouped into the East African Division, which was posted to India, landing at Calcutta,

Above: Dennis, standing, in a family group with his parents and brother Jim. 1936
Below: Dennis in the Royal Medical Corps. 1945

regrouped again, sent to Bangladesh, on to South East Asia and ended up in Burma. The Field Hospital was always behind the lines so we were not involved in the actual fighting. The injured were brought back to us and the severely injured were sent on to the General Hospital. My job was to ferry them back to the General Hospital and responsible for bringing back the food supplies. The Field Hospital moved up as the troops moved forward until we reached Rangoon, which was recaptured.

It was at that time we heard over the radio that the Americans had dropped an atom bomb on Japan and very soon the war was over.

*Reg. **Did you have to stay there?***

Dennis. We had to stay for a while and then made our way back through South East Asia and back to India again to a transit camp. We moved from there to Nairobi in South East Africa. We waited there until we came back to England on a ship, landed at Southampton and travelled back to Aldershot to be demobbed, when I was given my new 'civvy' suit and trilby hat. That was in November 1946. I rejoined my parents who were then living at Manaton and I was able to get a job in the lignite mine at Bovey Tracey on maintenance work. They were going to close it so I moved to a timber yard in Bovey Tracey. Two brothers ran it bringing in great trees and sawing them into planks that were sent up country for cabinet making and so forth.

Father saw an advert in the paper for a handyman and gardener at Alleron, Loddiswell and so I came down here with them and started working at Lilwell for you, that was 1948. Father then went to work for Luscombes, the Auctioneers and as you wished me to continue working at Lilwell I moved in and lodged with Mabel Rundle at Cross Farm.

I stayed with you for a while and then in 1949 Charlie Tarr said there was a job vacant at Torr Quarry, which I took.

When I started at Torr Quarry I was taking off the heading soil to get to the clean stone for blasting. Then the company bought a new plant, which was sited down the bottom of the pit, and I went there and worked under the stone bin loading up the trucks which ran on rails to be pulled up to the top plant by wire rope and winch. They continued with this method until it was scrapped when English China Clay (ECC) bought it and the stone was brought up by dumpers.

As I wasn't needed at the bottom of the quarry I was given a job with Cyril Brooking working on the tar plant making tar-macadam for road surfacing. I did that for several years until Bill Taylor retired and then I was given the job on the big crusher, controlling the heavy stones as they were fed into the crusher. They went on a conveyor belt up to bins into a secondary crusher to crush it smaller into chippings; these were graded into different sizes right down to dust and loaded as required. Some went to the tarmac plant which was alongside.

I retired under a Government Redundancy Scheme in the early 1970s before the quarry closed six months later in 1973. I wasn't allowed to work because I had this Government Pension so I just did odd jobs until I was 65 when I received a full Old Age Pension. Doris went around the village collecting National Savings, we met and starting courting. That was when I was lodging with Tom and Mabel Rundle at Cross Farm. Doris said, "If you want to see me you had better come to church, because I go to church on Sunday evenings." That was why I started going to church in Loddiswell.

We were married at Loddiswell Church in October 1952 by the Rev. George Bliss. He said to me one day you are a regular church goer. I would like you on the Parochial Church Council, and asked if I was confirmed and I said, "No I'm not." He said, "You will have to get confirmed." I joined the PCC and was appointed secretary as Mrs Tom Brooking had resigned.

After we were married Doreen was born and two years later David, both were christened by the Rev. Bliss. The Rev. Summerell followed the Rev. Bliss and a new rectory was built in Station Road as the parishes of Woodleigh and Loddiswell were to be combined. He appointed me to be a Church Warden in 1964 and I continued with those duties until 1995, when I retired as Warden and Secretary. For many years I taught at the Church Sunday School with Theo

Willing in the Lady Chapel before the morning services and when he died at an early age I continued for many years on my own, until about 1980.

Reg. *You have been involved with other village organisations?*

Dennis. I have been on the committee of the Loddiswell Playing Fields, the management of the Village Hall and the Over Sixties Club. I have shown vegetables and flower exhibits at Loddiswell Show for many years between 1950 and 2001 and won many prizes including the Silver Cup twice.

Below: Doris and Winnie Seldon in the chorus of the Cinderella pantomime at Kingsbridge Town Hall. 1940

Reg. *Doris, you spent your early years living at Station Road.*

Doris. I was born in one of the terraced houses on the lower side of the road, which were later knocked down, and where the new houses and bungalows have been built. Our neighbours were, Mark and Mary Quick, Ern and Ethel Jerred, Alf and Flo Pile, and down over the steps near the path to Inkly-Crinkly lived Lionel and Maud Ryder and their family. The Emmetts lived at Sunnydene and Tom Soper, his wife, Ethel and family of Margaret and Connie lived on the higher side of the road towards the well in Well Street. Sid and Martha Hine, Jack Freeman and Charlie Watts and their families all lived on the higher side and Wilf Burman and his wife Elsie on the lower side, all near Lod's Well.

We lived with my Grandfather, Albert Taylor and my Mother Bessie who had married my Father, Albert Elliott from Aveton Gifford. I was born in Station Road and also my sisters Joan and Phyllis. Later in life Joan married Bill Brooking and Phyllis married Ern Robinson.

The Council houses in New Road were built in 1927-28 and some of the people from Station Road moved over here. We were living here when Russell Edgecombe of Aveton Gifford rebuilt the Congregational Hall in 1930. Some of the first families that moved into New Road were George Brooking, Ethel Soper, Lionel Ryder and my Grandfather, Albert Taylor, and our family. In those days there wasn't any traffic going up and down New Road because, at the bottom end, there was a fence with a kissing gate in it and all the traffic had to go up around the school. Right opposite our houses there were steps going right up to the school and we used to slip home in playtime to get a drink and something to eat. There were big families living in these houses then, George Brooking's children were Bill, who married my sister Joan, Tom, Georgette, Evelyn, Marjorie, Roy, Cyril and Myrtle.

In those days there were no buses, so if we wanted to go to Kingsbridge we could walk and hope somebody may give us a lift or go down to the station and catch the train. Our shopping was done in the village at Yallands at the London

House Stores or Elliotts; both shops had bakeries and made their own bread. Butter and lard came in great blocks and would be cut down to what was wanted. Sugar had to be weighed up 'cus that came in great bags. Salt was in bars, great hard salt, you had to have a hammer to knock it up. Monday was always washing day, we used to have a wooden trough, which we put outside to put it soaking on Saturday night. We used soda to get the stains out and scrubbed it with bars of Puritan soap; there wasn't any powder then. Ironing was done on Mondays if it was dry otherwise 'twas left 'til next day. Cleaning the house was done every day. I left school when I was 14 and went to work at Alleron for Mrs Wise, she was blind and her daughters were Stella, Betty and Mrs Fleming, I can't remember her Christian name. Then there was a son Lancelot who lived up in Scotland. I then moved to Blackwell Parks for Capt. and Mrs Conran just before the war. I remember one day Capt. Conran was outside and shouted, "There are some enemy planes, they've just flown down the valley," and we heard the bombing of Aveton Gifford. I walked from Loddiswell to Blackwell Parks and back every day of the week including Sundays until I was married in 1952.

Reg. I remember you were one of the main collectors for National Saving for the war effort!

Doris. Yes, I collected all around the village; I did that all through the war; if people were not at home they would leave the money where I could find it. I have belonged to the Women's Institute and to the Over Sixties Club for many years and enjoyed it.

Below: Judges at Loddiswell's VE Day celebrations 1995. Left to right: Cyril Brooking, Capt. William Peek and Dennis Sharland.

Gwen Seldon

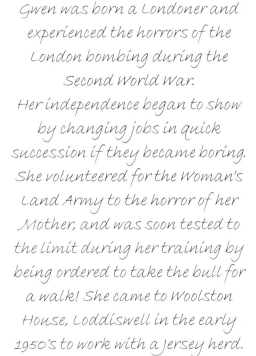

Soon after this interview Gwen became ill and she passed on to join her beloved Bill in March 2003. Her cheerfulness and spontaneous laughter endeared her to all who knew her.

*R*eg. *Gwen Seldon lives at Torr View and I have come to talk to her about her life in Loddiswell. Gwen, You have lived here for many years!*

Gwen. Yes, 48 years, I came here in 1954 and Bill and I were married in 1955. I was a Londoner, born in Hackney in 1929 and then lived at Stoke Newington. I went to Newington Green School, where my Father was a caretaker, until I was ten and was fortunate to have the whole playground to play with my friends. We had plenty of room to roller skate as there was a slope and we could skate down, bump into the bottom wall and almost knock ourselves out but we immediately had another go. We played whip and top, ball games, hop scotch and five stones. In that game we had to throw a stone in the air, pick another up and catch the first one before it fell to the ground. Some of the roads around us were busy mainly with horses and carts. The coal man had a four-wheeled wagon pulled by a Shire horse, and I remember the man who came around with the barrel organ with his monkey on top. He provided

Gwen was born a Londoner and experienced the horrors of the London bombing during the Second World War.
Her independence began to show by changing jobs in quick succession if they became boring. She volunteered for the Woman's Land Army to the horror of her Mother, and was soon tested to the limit during her training by being ordered to take the bull for a walk! She came to Woolston House, Loddiswell in the early 1950's to work with a Jersey herd. After marrying Bill she made her home in the village.

entertainment and collected our pennies in his cap. The scissors grinder came around on his three-wheeled bike. Milk was delivered right to the school: we all had to have our third of a pint of milk and a spoonful of the dreaded cod liver oil. From time to time 'Nitty Nora' would visit the school to inspect our heads for lice.

When the war started my Father was called up into the Navy and my eldest sister had joined the Women's Royal Naval Service (WRNS). Then the school was evacuated to Wales because of the war but I didn't go with the main school. I went with Myrtle, my second older sister, who was at a business school at Welford in Northamptonshire; Mother thought she would look after me. I hated it because there wasn't anyone there of my age, they were all in their 'teens. There was an army camp near by and she would go off with her friends dancing and I was left on my own. I did not settle down and came back to my Mother's who still lived at the school.

Unfortunately the bombing then started and we were bombed out. Enemy planes dropped high explosive bombs and on a couple of nights we went down into the Anderson shelter but it was so damp and miserable. We were allowed to go over to the Mildmay Club, the mother club of all the working men's clubs, and sleep under the billiard table. I spent a lot of time in the Club and didn't do any schooling. Dad was worried about this; he was stationed down at HMS Collingwood at Gosport. He said it is pretty quiet there so we all moved down. We were only there a week and they started bombing Portsmouth so I was pushed from school to school until I was 14.

We returned to London and then the V1's, or doodlebugs, started dropping. I got a job at Manor Gardens in the National Savings office but we were bombed out of there with a doodlebug. One could hear them coming and when the motor cut out we would hold our breath until you heard the 'crump' as they blew up. Later the V2s came over, they were rockets and you couldn't hear them coming until they exploded. I was in London and it was very frightening; eventually we worked in the basement of Manor Gardens filing away National Savings Certificates. I was bored to tears and I went to work on the switchboard at my Sister's place in the City dealing with Imports and Exports.

I became friendly with two girls and we used to go to the Lyceum Club dancing afternoons and evenings, we had a great time. On Sundays we would go to Hyde Park or St James's Park, and we were in London for the VE Day Celebrations, that was a great day, I didn't sleep for 48 hours! My two friends at Manor Gardens said they wanted to join the Women's Land Army, that was in 1948. So we went to get our Medical and I was the only one that passed. When I told my parents Mother was livid. I had my papers to do six weeks training at Shimpling, near Bury St. Edmunds, milking cows.

Reg. **What was your impression as a London girl when you came in contact with these great animals?**

Gwen. It was all right until I had to take the bull for a walk! The head cowman said "It is about time you learnt how to take the bull for a walk." I looked at him and said "Hey !" He came with

me and we led the bull, a great big Red Poll, with a wooden staff to the ring in his nose.

My job was mainly feeding the young bullocks. I used to carry a bag of food out into the field and they became so excited I was often pushed into the 'blimin' trough until I learnt how to shout and bawl at them!

I was then sent to Sainsbury's Farm at a place called Hadleigh in Suffolk where they kept Ayrshires, it was a place I loved. We were three London girls and lived in a thatched cottage on our own and looked after ourselves.

It was a bit of a surprise to find we had to use bucket toilets at the bottom of the garden, we had the best rhubarb in the district. .We had oil

Above: Gwen with the Ayrshire cow, Twinkle being shown for Sainsbury's Farms, Hadleigh, Suffolk. 1949

lamps and cooked with an oil stove but we had a fabulous time, we cycled everywhere. I was there for two and a half years until my 21st birthday and then the Women's Land Army was disbanded, but I had the bug by that time.

I went home and couldn't find a job and I thought I'm not going back to office work. I saw in the Dairy Farmer magazine a job advertised in Loddiswell with Mr Pratt at Woolston House. He must have lived there for four or five years because, before me, he had two Land Army girls who had left and both had married local Veterinary Surgeons. Mr. Pratt drove a great big white Jaguar and Mrs Pratt had a little Sports car an MG.

Gladys Bailey was there when I arrived, she was

a dynamic person, I used to struggle with a bale of straw, she would come along, pick it up and chuck it like it was a paper bag. We kept Jersey cows and milked them in the cowshed, we bottled the milk in the dairy and it was collected by Dawe's Creameries.

We cut some hay and had Frank Lilley to help, he worked for your Father at Woolston Farm, and unfortunately he always appeared to be sick when it was haymaking time. Arthur and Phyllis Kent lived at the Lodge and he looked after the pig herd, Ken LeGrice was the gardener, they all used to come in to help.

I was there for two years when I had a heck of a row with Gladys and I walked out and went back to London. I joined my sister who was working in the NAAFI in the R.A.F. Camp at Halton, Buckinghamshire and stayed there for twelve months.

I was transferred to a place near Oxford, a big army camp when Mrs Pratt wrote to my Mother

Above: The Jersey herd at Woolston House, Loddiswell. 1950
Below: Bottling milk at Woolston House.

asking if I would like to come back as no one else could get on with Gladys. I said I would come back but not live in the House but would live in the village. I lodged with Marion Shepherd who lived in No 18 Ashwood Park and used to go to dances with her sister Amber. That is where I met Bill; she had finished his army service but was still on emergency reserve. He was working down at the concrete works at New Mill with Reg Finnamore making blocks. He was there for about two years when Raymond Ryder said they needed another man on the Water Board so Bill joined them. He worked there for 25 years when unfortunately he was laid off because of asthma so he took early retirement at the age of 57.

Bill's Father came down with Northcotts at the same time as Arthur Grant when Rake Quarry was opened. He was a very skilled blacksmith and tempered the picks and drills for the quarrymen. Bill hated that job but his brother Arthur took to it and went down to New Quarry, Launceston. He was unfortunately killed in a motor accident in 1985.

When I became engaged to Bill I left Woolston House and went to work at Coombe Royal, the old people's home and continued there until 1960. I enjoyed it, they were good fun. Then in 1961 I went down to Topsham Bridge with Mrs Hawker until 1971. When I left there I joined the Home Help Service and continued with the Service until 1989 when I was 60.

When I retired we had this marvellous trip out to Australia to see Bill's sister Rose who lives in Perth: she had married Michael Moore from Mounts, East Allington. We stayed a week in Hong Kong, then over to Perth for a fortnight, travelling in the outback, which was lovely. Then we flew the four-hour journey to Sydney and had a week with her son Kevin. We flew up to Cairns and on to Darwin for another week before Singapore for three days and then home. Bill always loved his garden and was happy at home; I did however get him to go to Malta and we went to Scotland for several years. Since Bill's been gone I continue to go to the Over Sixties and I enjoy reading and crosswords, it helps to my keep my brain active.

Wally and Hettie Tarr

Reg. I have come to talk to Wally and Hettie Tarr at Inner Weeke after coming over the saddleback hill by Outer Weeke. Have you always lived here Wally?

Wally. Yes, I was born here at Inner Weeke but when I was seven years old we moved to Outer Weeke and back here again when we were married in 1953.

In the early days everything was done by hand, cows were milked by hand and horses did all the land work until after the Second World War when tractors came in. We had twelve South Devon cows and a couple of carthorses to do the ploughing and all the cultivations.

Father grew a field of oats and a field of barley. The oats were fed to the stock and the straw used for feeding, some of the barley was sold and some fed to the stock. We grew a few swedes but no kale in those days. Hoeing the root crops took more labour and Cyril Harding used to come down to help, usually three days a week and then in the evenings a couple from Loddiswell, Charlie Tarr and Frank Quick, used to come to help with the hoeing and hay harvest, they used to enjoy it so long as they had some cider.

Wally is a true member of the farming community, born and lived at Weeke all his life. He has observed the changing pattern of agriculture turn full circle. His unconcerned and reflective attitude to scientific ways of farming has enabled him to live in a more relaxed and stress free environment. Both he and Hettie enjoy the pleasures of farming without the hassle the larger commercial farmers have experienced.

We pitched the hay onto a wagon and from there up on to the rick as it got higher. Father thatched the corn ricks but the hay ricks were always covered with galvanised iron. In the wintertime I had to go out with the horse and wagon and cut it out with a hay knife to take it back to the barn.

I started school at Aveton Gifford; I used to go out to Knap Mill and ride with Laskey Elliott in a pony and trap. When we got older we used to walk. Then Colin and I were taken away from Aveton Gifford and we went to Loddiswell for about twelve months and then into Kingsbridge to the Modern Secondary School, the one they've just knocked down in Fosse Road.

When I was eleven I was considered to be old enough and big enough to cycle to Loddiswell Station before school each day with the clotted cream. I carried it in a basket on the front of the bike and I had to catch the 7.40 am train; I only missed it once when I had a puncture. On Sundays I took the cream to Sorley Green to go by bus to Totnes, and then on by train to a cafe in Teignmouth.

Then the war came and put a stop to that. I left

school when I was 14 at Easter in 1940 and came home to help my Father until 1944.

I was called up to go down the mines, one of the Bevan Boys, and I kicked against it. I said I would go in any of the Services, preferably the army, but as I was on the land I got exempted. In the meantime Father had let Inner Weeke to Mr Rendle who had come from the Evacuation Area at Torcross and I had to go out to work two days a week, as we didn't have enough land.

I went over to Hatch for two days a week for Mr. Herman Hosking but he died and his son Bill took over. He eventually went down to Bowcombe, Ugborough and I helped him move there in 1951. Then I helped Jack Baker with his threshing tackle during the wintertime, but if Father was busy I stayed home. We milked cows until the bulk tankers came in and the churns went out, and now I keep a few store bullocks.

Reg. You were in the Home Guard!

Wally. Yes, I was in the Home Guard. I suppose it is a story, but children are different now. When we were younger we were not allowed to go up Loddiswell very often, that was the way with old parents in those days, so I put me age on to join the Home Guard, you had to be 16. I went to see Sid Scoble and he said, " How old are you?" and I said "Sixteen Sir." So I got in and went on parades and that sort of thing, and I was able to get up the village a bit more.

There were two pubs, the Turks Head and the New Bridge Inn. In those days it was all Loddiswell people, we knew everybody, now that's gone, a lot of people have come in. I remember Tom Rundle, Harry Withers, Lionel Ryder, Percy Ryder, Mr Scoble, Bill Yabsley, the majority went to the lower pub to play darts and euchre. They had teams that played other pubs around the area but I don't know about it now. Ern Luscombe used to ride his pushbike mornings from Aveton Gifford to Rake Corner to catch the lorry going to Torr and on a Sunday morning I used to go for a ride on my pushbike over to Hatch Bridge. Ern was often there and I'd say, "What be 'e doing then?" He would then ride over to the corner and back and if 'twas all right he would stop on the bridge and say, "There's a salmon down under there!"

Reg. Did you see the salmon?

Wally. Well, no, not until there was a knock on the door.

I remember another time when I was out the top of Great Gate catching rabbits with Frank Widger. We were up over the woods looking down and two Loddiswell men were by the river and Frank said to me, "What are they doing down there?" I said, "They'm after a fish!" We watched and I said, "I'm going to stay here." He said "What are you waiting for?" and I said, "You wait and see." Soon one came up through the woods with a salmon, he stopped and scrapped back some leaves and stuffed it in a rabbit's hole and covered it up. Eventually they disappeared and we couldn't see them for a while until they were further down the river. I said to Frank." Lets have a bash, I'm going down." I went down and scrapped back the leaves, stuck the salmon in a bag and was gone, 'course they could never say anything about it. Frank said he would never have believed it. There were a few people in Loddiswell who were dab hands at taking out salmon but now I don't think there is much of that, there are not the salmon about, I haven't seen one for a long time.

The other day Hettie and I were looking in our little stream, the Aller; and there was a shoal of little fish about four inches long and I think they were young salmon. The salmon must have gone up and spawned, and these were on their way back out to sea. After so many years they will come back.

Reg. Hettie, when did you come to this part of the country?

Hettie. I was born in the Fen Country on my Grandfather's farm in Huntingdonshire which is now Cambridgeshire. I was born there because my Father was away and my Aunt was a midwife, so my Mother only went back to have me. My Father was a chauffeur looking after a fleet of Daimler cars for a business man who lived in a big house, not really a stately home.

The countryside around was flat with good black soil growing corn, sugar beet, potatoes and celery; they grew a lot of celery. The sugar beet went to a factory in Peterborough.

I went to school in Peterborough and when I

was 16 I did a year's practical experience on a mixed farm in Northamptonshire. The owner was the Chairman of the Area War Agricultural Committee, his farming was ahead of the times, he already made silage.

I then went to an agricultural college for a year and then I came down here to a farm at Dartington Hall Trust in 1946. I was at Parsonage Farm where the Manager was Mr. Hawtin. Then I worked at East Worthel, near Westlake, Ermington for two and a half years before moving to East Cornworthy. We could hear the loud speakers from the paddle steamers as they plied up and down the River Dart.

I milked the South Devon cows by hand, there were about a dozen, this took quite a while twice a day. I had itchy feet when I was young, so I moved about a lot. I came to Loddiswell and worked for the Winzers at Greatgate Farm and was there until their son David came home and I had to get another job for six months before I married Wally.

We were married in September, 1953 and moved to Inner Weeke, which had been empty for a couple of years after Mr Rendle left. We had no electricity here and it wasn't until 1962 that electricity was brought in. We managed with candles and oil lamps and made the best of it.

Reg. You did not come here just to milk the cows!

Hettie. I didn't do a lot of milking but I used to get roped in for the ones that kicked. I remember Nancy; I certainly remember Nancy, Caw!! I missed the cows, though; because when the bulk tankers came in we gave up milking. We then bought my first Jersey cow in October 1976 and hand milked her and subsequent ones for the next 20 years, I always liked hand milking.

I fed the calves and we had poultry and geese. Eggs used to go to the South Hams Packing Station in Loddiswell, Ivan Pope or Ivor King collected them. At harvest time I took 'drinkings' out in the fields, sandwiches, homemade buns and a kettle of hot tea.

Reg. When were the children born?

Hettie. Linda was born twelve months after we were married, then three years and a bit later Judith and after another two years Richard. They have turned out well, we are pleased with them. They all went to Loddiswell School and on to Kingsbridge Comprehensive School.

Reg. None of them went farming?

Hettie. Judith was mad about poultry, when she was thirteen she was allowed to work and went up to the Cassidy's picking up eggs. When she left school she went to Harper Adams Agricultural College; she did a sandwich course, a year at the college and then she went to America for a year on a farm and then back for another year to do a HND Course in General Agriculture.

She is now married with two children and still works on a poultry farm, which she is able to do with the children. Linda is in Staffordshire, she did a business course at Torquay Technical College, started work at Michael Locke's in Kingsbridge and then she went to London dealing with business portfolios, she has three girls. Richard went to Torquay Tech. and after leaving there went to North Devon to J & S Marine at Barnstaple. He moved to Marconi, then Plessey and from there he went to Paris, still with Plessey, and he is still there working in telecommunications. It's quite beyond us,

Left: Hettie with the old pump at Inner Weeke Farm.

Left: Flete House "I went to Flete doing domestic work; the Hon. Mrs Peek was one who lived there. It was a bit of a shock to the system as I had been mucking out pigs here on the farm..."

circuit boards and that.

None of them came home on the farm, it wasn't big enough as it was only 35 acres, it wasn't even viable for us, we both went out to work in the end.

I went to Flete doing domestic work; the Hon. Mrs Peek was one who lived there. It was a bit of a shock to the system as I had been mucking out pigs here on the farm and these ladies said, "Where did you work before?" They thought my present job was much better but I did not like being confined indoors, the central heating I found very trying but eventually I got used to it. It was good fun working with a lot of people and it was a beautiful place to work in, very regulated.

Years before Linda had been born at Flete when it was a Maternity Hospital that had been evacuated there from Plymouth during the war. It was only in the last week that I was there I found the room I was in, this was not surprising, as they had moved two of the partition walls.

The future of farming is very uncertain, small farms are disappearing and large farms are getting bigger, I am glad we are retiring and not just starting now. How do you start today unless you take on from your parents?

Farms are coming up to let and there seems to be very little interest in renting them.

Wally. I don't know what the outcome is going to be, no one seems to be able to see the way forward, you can see why a lot of farmer's sons don't want to take it on. We have lost M.A.F.F. and got D.E.F.R.A. run by a lot of politicians who haven't a clue. We don't want to go back to the 1930s when our parents had a struggle to live.

I remember hearing Father say, now I am not sure whether he bought cattle in the autumn and sold them in the spring, or bought 'um in the spring and sold them in the autumn, but he took them up to Brent, they went by train from Loddiswell Station, and whatever he gave for them that's what he sold them for. We don't want to see those days again

Below: Bert Tarr, Wally's Father, waiting for Cyril Harding to throw up the rope.

Roger and Joyce Lethbridge

Reg. I have come to No. 4 Vine Terrace, the home of Roger and Joyce Lethbridge. From 1860 to 1869 Vine Terrace was a malt house and belonged to the Willing family who emigrated to New Zealand. Then the property was converted into four terraced houses. When did you come here Roger?

Roger. We came here in 1995 from Tyepitte Cottage in the Courtledge. Three of my brothers and I were born at Churchlands, Modbury. My Father, Ern Lethbridge, moved from there to Frittiscombe, Stokenham when I was two, and my brother John and my two sisters were born there. He farmed there right up until the evacuation in 1943.

My Father was a threshing contractor with steam engines as well as being a farmer. In December 1943 we moved out because of the evacuation of the area and went to live with Uncle William Lethbridge at Coombe, Loddiswell and stayed there during the nine months of the evacuation. Everything had to be moved, all the equipment, the cows were milked at Coombe for the next three months and then Father sold it all off.

I remember we took two traction engines to

Roger experienced many years operating a threshing machine but as combine harvesters took over he enjoyed the mechanical side of farming. Owing to ill health he had to take a more sedate job driving a hire car. Joyce was involved in the village in her early life, later working in the South Hams Packing Station. They have been staunch supporters of our village community, always willing to help and taking great pleasure in doing so.

Coombe, there was a Marshall engine and a Burrell Twin and Mr E Noyce cut them up for scrap iron as metal was scarce and needed for armaments for the war; 'twas a great shame.

During the time we were there a great tragedy happened. My brother John was playing in the fields with his two mates on a Sunday afternoon in May 1944. They found an anti-tank bomb, which the Americans had left in a rabbit's hole as they travelled through the area on their way to embarkation for the Normandy landings. One of the boys threw it at the gatepost and two of them were killed. Desmond Martin had the flesh blown off his legs as he was the nearest to the explosion. My brother John was standing at one side got caught in the chest and was killed outright. One of his mates called, Stafford Auger, had to have his leg amputated, and he died the next day. I was fourteen when we were at Coombe and I helped my Father with a bit of contracting before we went back to Stancombe, Sherford in October 1944. The farm there was in an awful state, it had been empty for nine months and was all grown in with weeds and kale stumps; we had to cut it all off

Above: Roger's Father, Ern with his horse and wain.

and burn it.

The place was full of hand grenades, hundreds all over the place in the hedges and fields; we had to get the police nearly every day to remove them. It should have been cleared before we went back but it wasn't, it was highly dangerous. We continued there until 1948 when Father retired to a house in Stokenham village. I was 19 then so I took over one of the threshing sets, travelling around the farms in the district until 1954. I had a tractor, an International W9 that replaced the steam engines. Father had bought it new in about 1940 under the Marshall Aid Importation's from the USA. It came in boxes, they had to be assembled at Newton Abbot.

Joyce and I were married in 1954 at Loddiswell Church and moved to North Efford, Aveton Gifford. I took the threshing tackle and covered an area around Aveton Gifford. Uncle Jack Baker threshed at most of the farms in the Loddiswell area and another Uncle, Alan Baker went out to the Bigbury side. I did that until we moved to Cornwall in 1957, to farm in the St Germans district on the Bake Estate, it was mainly dairying, 20 cows on 90 acres. At that time that was the normal size for a dairy herd. We were renting the farm but the rent was too high and there was no room for expansion.

After about eight years I saw a man, a Mr. Sampson advertising for a tractor driver in Loddiswell. I rang him up one afternoon and you

Below: Planting vines at Lilwell in 1977.

took me on. When I started at Lilwell you had about 350 acres. Fred Diamond was the cowman, Leonard Wood looked after the large pig herd and Harold Eastley did general farm work. Eventually his two sons Roger and Alan came to work on the farm. It was quite a big business and all those men working on the farm. On the farm today you can divide that labour force by four.

Reg. At that time we still had the large flocks of free-range poultry.

Roger. All very labour intensive. I used to help collecting the eggs and you had day old chicks for sale, and reared four to eight weeks old pullet chicks for customers. You had your own hatchery. I was mainly involved with the arable side, ploughing in the winter, cultivating, hedge trimming and combine harvesting. We had a Massey 760 Combine at first and then we went on to a Clayson. In the first few years I was there we grew a 160 acres of barley and, of course we did the silage and hay for the cows. In the winter I helped look after the beef cattle at Stanton.

During the last week I was there we started planting vines. I used the borer to make the deep holes for the vines and you and Harold were putting them in, that was in May 1977.

I stayed at Lilwell until 1977 when I developed heart trouble and I had to leave the land. When I gave up farm work I had to take a lighter occupation and I went down to the Skill Centre and trained in engineering. Then I took a job at Brown Sharpe in Plympton in a factory where they made big cylinders for hydraulic rams used in trailers, lorries and North Sea oilrigs. That was all the firm did, employing about 60 men.

Eventually after 18 months I couldn't put up with the noise, having always been accustomed to working outdoors so I applied for a job in Kingsbridge driving a taxi and the hearse when required, for Wills Garage. That was October 1979 until I was made redundant four and a half years later.

I was then able to work for John D. Andrews, the Undertaker, attending funerals and making coffins, but eventually owing to my heart condition I found it difficult cleaning the vehicles so I retired at the age of 60.

Reg. You have had a lot of pleasure since your retirement.

Roger. Yes, playing euchre and whist three or four times a week, it keeps my brain active and I enjoy it. We have belonged to the Over Sixties for several years, where we have over 90 members at present. We have a meeting nearly every week in the Village Hall.

Reg. Joyce I remember when you were young you lived opposite the Village Primary School

Joyce. Yes, that's right. I remember getting the keys from Mrs Bob Hine, the Caretaker, who lived at the lower end of the Bank and giving them to the Teacher to unlock the School. I always enjoyed school with Miss Michell and Miss Common. We did sewing and art as well as the main lessons, but my best subject was arithmetic.

I was born in 1929 and was ten years old when there was a threat of war. Just before that I was standing in the playground and saw a plane fly over very low with a swastika on the side, it was as plain as anything but we did not know what a swastika was then. It must have been a spy plane surveying the area.

I went to Kingsbridge School when I was eleven in 1940. We went by Clark's coach but as there were so many evacuees the coach had to travel twice. If you got on the first coach in the morning you were dropped at Stentiford Hill and had to walk down the steep hill to Wallingford Road and up to the School. In the evening it was vice-versa.

One Saturday morning a bomb went through the School, which was lucky as it was a Saturday morning when no children were there. I have recently learned that a bomb was dropped at the Grammar School at Westville at the same time. It went through the Hall, the Headmaster's room and exploded across the road and demolished two houses. We had to have our lessons at the Congregational Hall at Loddiswell for three weeks as our school had been damaged. All the children had to go to school in their own villages. After that there was another raid and they said 'that's Loddiswell this time' and we were terrified, but it was the raid on Aveton Gifford.

118

I had to register when I was 16, but the war was over by then in 1945. I aimed for the WRAF but I was not called up. Since I was fourteen I had been working at the South Hams Packing Station. I had a break for twelve months, working in the office of the Regal Cinema but as there were no regular buses in those days I had to walk home. I was always terrified walking up through the trees at Coombe Royal when other people were walking up and down and I didn't know who they were. I was terrified so I thought 'I can't stand this' so I went back to the Packing Station.

We were married in 1954 at Loddiswell Church and lived for three years at North Efford across the Stakes at Aveton Gifford. Ann was born in 1955. When she was a toddler we were always afraid of her going in the mud and water of the estuary. During the time we were there we saw many people stuck on the mud, and cars, trying to come through the deep water, would stall and they would climb on the roof shouting for help. On one occasion George Coaker's speedboat

Below: The weekly whist drives at Loddiswell village hall. "What is Kathy Brooking going to play next?" watched by Joyce and Roger Lethbridge and Jean Tarr.

misjudged the tide going out and got stuck on the mud.

Peter was born in 1956 and Andrew in 1962 when we were living in Cornwall.

Reg. You have been involved in many of the village organisations!

Joyce. I was a member of the Tennis Club, a treasurer of the WI for twelve years and also treasurer of the Loddiswell Village Hall committee for twelve years, I've just passed that over to Rachael Tate. In the Over Sixties I have run a Thrift Club: the Members pay me each week and have the money out at Christmas. The most we have had was £5,600 in a year. You should see their faces at Christmas when they draw it out, delighted they are.

I attend sales at the Market Hall in Kingsbridge. My job on viewing days is just to stand around and see that we don't loose anything and on the day of the sale I check things out.

I've enjoyed our retirement. Sometimes we go into the Rest Centre at Kingsbridge and have coffee. We sit and listen to all sorts of tales. John Tucker who used to farm at Venn is over 90 and tells some good stories. John Morris spent years in the Navy, and John Deem is another one, all with good stories to tell of years ago.

Ned and Hazel Lethbridge

*R*eg. *I am at 24 Ashwood Park to meet Ned and Hazel Lethbridge. Have you always lived in Loddiswell, Ned?*

Ned. I used to live at No. 1 Vine Terrace, that's where I was born in 1934. Granfer George Lethbridge and Gran lived in No.3 and when Granfer died we moved in there with Gran during her lifetime and then into Vine Cottage. I went to school in Loddiswell but didn't like it and ran home a lot. Miss Common and Miss Michell were the teachers then. I got home one day and had only just arrived when the Attendance Officer called. I had to go back next morning and hold me hand out to have the cane.

As there were so many evacuees some of us younger children had to go to the Church Hall with Miss Michell. When I was older two of us would go to Cyril Harding's at Little Reads and collect a little churn of milk, it had a handle each side and we brought it down to school. They dipped it out with a ladle for the children. I liked it at home, out in the garden feeding my

Ned's vivid account of his childhood days brings back memories of country life in the past. His love of working on the land gave him great enjoyment and kept him occupied in his spare time. This must have been a great blessing to his parents as there was always a mischievous streak ready to surface if the situation arose. His love of animals and gardening has continued throughout his life. Hazel portrays life as a Naval Officers daughter and since settling in Loddiswell she has helped to instigate many new social activities, which have continued to flourish.

rabbits, Father would bring home turnips, mangolds, flatpoles and corn when he was working down at Ham Farm for Mr. Alfred Hingston. When I was a little tacker, Tom Squires at Greystones Farm delivered coal around the village. He would sit me up on his coal wagon, black my face and we would go around the village with the horse and wagon delivering coal.

When I got bigger I spent a lot of time down at Ham Farm with my Father, especially in the holidays with Sylvia Hingston, and we would turn the separator handle to produce the cream. There was always a big dish of cream in the dairy with a spoon in it and we used to go in and help ourselves. Mr. Hingston would be out milking the cows and he would say "Come here boy," and I used to bend down and he would squirt the milk in my mouth! He had an open top sports car down in the barn and Sylvia and I used to go down there and play in it. When they left I never saw Sylvia again.

In those days the gypsies would sometimes

camp up at Ham Butts, they used to tie their ponies up and sit outside their caravans making clothes pegs. They would cut sticks from the hedges, split them and bind them around with a bit of tin, then they would come around the village with a basket on their arm selling them. We used to go up and terrify 'um and get 'um wicked, they used to chase us down by the Church and right across Courtledge.

I remember there was an old scissor grinder who would come around the village with a pedal grinder fixed to the side of a pram. He used to sharpen all the knives and scissors. He would come to Town's Lane and Gran would fill his pot with tea and he would sharpen her knives for nothing.

I went to Kingsbridge Secondary School and Father then went out to Reveton to work for Mr. Leonard Scobell. I liked to go out to Reveton to help; I remember planting potatoes and leading the horse to bank them in. Often Father and I would work on into the evening, scuffling and banking them up and the same with the turnips and mangolds.

Reg. **Farm staff usually had a row or two of potatoes in the farmer's field for themselves.**

Ned. Yes, two or three rows for ourselves and we did the work for the farmer's potatoes as well.

At harvest time I would lead the horse to pick up the sheaves of corn to take back to the rick and hold the horse steady while they were pitching them up on the rick. Later on we would take all the wheat sheaves to the barn to make reed and I used to go in the barn with them. We would pick up a sheaf and knock out the corn on a reed maker, a curved slatted bench, and then tie up a bundle of reed to a beam, all ear ends together and comb out all the grass from the stubble.

After harvest we would take a horse and cart or wagon and go around to the hedges and cut spear sticks. On a wet day we would go in the barn and Father would use a little hook to split the sticks down into spears and twist them. I've still got that little hook outside now.

The spears were all ready for thatching the ricks. Father would take up the bundles of reed; I wasn't big enough to do that. He would spread out the reed and I would be on the ladder passing the spears to him to hold it in place.

Then came threshing time when Bill Widger came in with his Ransome threshing machine pulled by an International W.9. I looked after the douse and liked catching the rats. Sometimes they used the elevator to take the loose straw into the barn or used the trusser to bundle it up. The neighbours used to come in to help, as ten or a dozen men were needed for the job. Father used to go to other farms nearby when they were threshing. I loved farming. Father said, "If I had enough money I'd buy you a farm."

We had a good life; at weekends all the family went for walks. Auntie and Uncle Andrews who lived in Fosse Road would come out from Kingsbridge and go to church here one week and we would walk in there the next Sunday. If 'twas a fine weekend we would walk down to Hatch Bridge, go down across the fields and play rounders there. Then if we were thirsty we would walk up to Churchstow and have a drink there and then walk home.

Some Sunday nights in the winter time we would walk to Aveton Gifford and go to church, then back across the bridge and up to Venn, back to Hatch Bridge and up the lane. I remember my cousin and Auntie Carrie, who lived at Peckham, didn't like the dark and he would strike matches all the way up the lane.

When my Mother, Betty Lethbridge, and Gladys Hodge took part in the village pantomimes they would always go into Bridge Inn and have a couple of sherries to steady their nerves, before they came up to the Hall.

I was 15 when I left school, I would like to have left before but we all had to go on to that age. I had a job with the Water Works, a firm at North Huish called Foster Deacon. I was with Percy Ryder, Lionel Ryder, Owen Ryder, Gerald Ryder, 'twas all Ryders in those days.

We started up at Churchstow where we dug the sewers and water pipe trenches for the Council houses there. It was all done by hand in those days, pick and shovel, all day long.

When I left there I went to work at the Concrete Works, down at New Mill. Glyn Brooking took me on and my job was making concrete troughs for farmers, concrete fencing posts, slabs and kerbs for the Council. They were made on a vibrating platform driven by an engine with a belt drive. I worked with Jim Hine who was in charge of that section, making all the reinforcements and the mould boxes, bending it to shape. Concrete blocks were made individually; the concrete came down a shute into a vibrating box on a stand and were pressed by a lever, which banged down on the top of it. When the lever was released the block would fly out and then had to be carried back on a plate to dry.

Several men worked there, Bill Stone, Bill Edgcombe, Reg Finnamore, Francis Lilley and Douglas Luscombe from Bigbury, who came on his motorbike and sidecar. I stayed there until the concrete business was transferred to Torr Quarry and I went there for a while before I

Below: Ned in the Royal Pioneer Corps. 1954 "I was in the Pioneers and worked at an underground depot shifting around ammunition."

went in the Army to do my National Service in 1952.

I was 18 when I went in and was sent to Wrexham to do my training. Then I was moved to a Working Camp in the Midlands where I stayed for two years. I was in the Pioneers and worked at an underground depot shifting around ammunition. They used to bring in big trucks and we had to load them. It was put on to carriages and pushed out to the trains, as they were not allowed to come into the store where the ammunition was kept. When the trains were loaded they would join the main line to go where it was wanted.

Reg. **Did you have a forklift?**

Ned. No, everything was done by hand; it was all stacked up, miles long, shells and small ammunition.

We were taken to work by train from the camp to the depot each morning and brought back by train at night. There were Polish chaps there who cooked our meals, they were good cooks and the food was beautiful.

After two years I was demobbed and went to work for Scobles the builders in Kingsbridge. John Webber, Basil Taylor and several others were there in those days. I did the labouring for the council houses up at East Allington in 1956, and I stayed with the company until they closed down. That was the year, 1956, when I met Hazel.

Reg. **How did that happen?**

Ned. I was up in the telephone box. I'd come out of church and I came out of the telephone box and Hazel was outside. We started talking and she jumped in my car and away we went.

Reg. **Oh, I see!**

Ned. Several of us used to meet up there and sometimes we would run down through the village, knocking on everybody's doors. We would split up when we got to Butcher Walke's, some would go down New Road and we would meet up down at the New Bridge Inn, to see everybody looking out their doors.

When Scobles closed down, I was home here on the dole, walking around the village with no work to do. One day Harold Joint came down through the village and said "Got no job?" I said,

Above: Onions galore, Ned's pride and joy! "I love my garden and ... three gardens keep me going."

"No" and he said, "You can come out with me, my man's home bad." That was old Wilf Burman so I went out with Harold and poor old Burman didn't come back, he died. I stayed out at Wigford with Harold for ten years. One morning I was going up Terrace Hill to work and met John Webber and Basil Taylor and they asked if I would like to come back on the building job and I jumped at it. I started with them and was with them for 20 years. Eventually I couldn't climb ladders, as I could not go up heights, it happened all of a sudden. When I went to the doctor he said I must get a job on the ground.

My son Ian, was working with the National Trust at the time so I was able to get a job with them working on the coastal footpaths for a few years. When they bought Buckland Abbey they wanted a crowd of us to go down there and three of us laid all those cobblestones around the Abbey. I used to go to and fro every day. When we had finished the National Trust was cutting down on staff and a gardening job at Sharpitor, Salcombe came up. I applied for it and got it. I believe there were about 30 people who applied for it and I was the lucky one. I stayed there nine years until I retired at the age of 64.

Reg. Since your retirement what do you like doing?

Ned. I've still got four rabbits, which keeps me happy. Years ago I used to compete in the Fur and Feather Show held monthly in the village hall and I took several prizes. I kept Silver Foxes, Californians, and New Zealand Whites, Dutch and Rex. I kept these for Show. I've got a new one now called 'Lion Head'. The first I ever had came from a jumble sale down at the school and I think it was Jack Eastley who gave them for sale. My Gran bought them for me and I've had rabbits ever since. The most I've ever had was 21 which I reared for meat, and the money I made from rabbits bought the furniture when we were married.

I love my garden and I do my Sister Thelma's, and Chrissie Edgecombe's who is nearly 90. The three gardens keep me going.

Reg. I know you are a keen gardener. Everyone admires your display of vegetables in the belfry for the Church Harvest Festival.

Ned. I started bell ringing when I was 14 and Freddie Kernick was in charge. He said, "You are too small", anyway Fred Parscliffe came along and took on the captaincy and he said, "Come right over." I have rung for 54 years and I still ring in the team now. I have wound the church clock for just over 30 years. I don't like sitting at home, I'm not keen on television, I don't watch much of that, and bingo would drive me right up the wall! I like to have a talk with me neighbours over the fence.

Reg. I remember you were in my Sunday school class in the days of the Rev. George Bliss, and you were always the joker who would set the class laughing. One look from the Rev. Bliss and order was restored.

Ned. I liked old Parson Bliss, he was a good fellow. When he married my sister, he kept them up the altar talking to them and he said, "The chimney will smoke and the clothes line will break." He came up one morning for communion and couldn't get in the church. Johnny Brown had the key and he went over and knocked him up, I can see him now, he stood in the road and shouted up " Brown, are you dead!"

Reg. Hazel, when were you married? I remember your maiden name was Butler.

Hazel. We were married in 1960 and my family were the first to live in this house when it was built. I was born in Great Bookham, Surrey where we used to live in No. 1 School Lane, right opposite the school. My first memory is of being taken down to the Air Raid shelter in the school ground, a big shelter. We all sat in there in the dark and we used to sing songs. I was about four years old then.

My Father was in the Navy in Plymouth and we came down to a two bed-roomed cottage at Stoke Fleming. We did not have any electricity, only oil lamps and candles, no water inside, we had to go about a hundred yards up the road and pump the water in buckets to carry home. Bath night was once a week in front of the Lidstone stove in a great big tin bath which we all shared,

Above: The Butler family, 1949. Left to Right: Barbara, Rose, Hazel, Derek and Mother.

just topping the water up.

I had two older sisters and a younger brother. I used to sleep in a single bed with my sister, one each way, head to toe. I remember first seeing my Father; it sounds silly now, but we used to sleep in a big front room. Mum used to have the double bed with my little brother in it and our single bed was next to it. One morning I woke up and said to my sister "There's a stranger sleeping with Mummy." She said, " Don't be silly, that's Daddy". I could never remember seeing him before, because he had been away for two and a half years in the Navy. He gave us a cuddle and took us downstairs and gave us a bunch of bananas, which were very rare then. He gave me this banana and I started eating it, but he said, "You have got to peel it first." I had never seen a banana before; they were unobtainable in the war years. When I started school at Stoke Fleming I remember we had to have a third of a pint of milk and a spoon of cod liver oil every day before our dinner, we hated it! I went there until I was ten and then we came here in 1952. That was the first time we had any electricity and indoor water supply. It was luxury, we had an indoor toilet, a real luxury. Mother and Father came to see it as Rodgers of Holbeton was building it.

I went to Loddiswell School for a couple of terms with Miss Michell, Miss Common, and Miss Todd who went on to Kingsbridge and taught me there. When I left school at 15 I went to Grey's Cafe, Kingsbridge for about two years and then back here to the South Hams Packing Station. I remember going to the Devon County Show where we had a stand displaying the produce we sold.

I was there quite a few years before going to the London House Stores where I worked for 30 years. I started there with the Davies doing the paper round at first. Then Mr. Vascalini took over and later Ken and Sylvia Pridham, followed by John and Pearl Lewis and then Michael and Mary Piggott. I left there in 1996 and went into Fourbuoys, the newsagents in Kingsbridge for a couple of years before I retired.

Reg. You did a lot for the Over Sixties

Hazel. Yes, we started it 23 years ago; there were three of us, Margaret Rundle, Anita Hinton and myself. We were talking one morning and thought it would be a good idea for the older people in the village to get together once a week to have a cup of tea and a chat. We sent little notes around to everyone and we had our first meeting in December 1979; since it was formed it has grown and grown. Walter Hine was the secretary for many years and arranged the speakers before Susan Freeman took over.

I helped to start the short mat bowling which is now a thriving club. I have always been interested in knitting and crocheting and just recently I have done some patchwork quilting; I do like to use my hands. I enjoy tapestry work and did some kneelers in the church.

Our hand bell ringers play in the church and chapel on special occasions and sometimes at weddings. I think we've been ringing together for 25 years or it may be more. I've always enjoyed the weekend rallies when we have travelled to different parts of the country.

Reg. What about bingo?

Hazel. I love that and Ian, our son, is a caller with Gordon Beckley. Years ago we used to have carnivals in the village; we all loved dressing up with our fancy hats and dresses. My Father Jack Butler, did a lot towards the arrangements and he loved the dancing in the evenings. Only recently I came across one of my Father's letters when he was in the Navy, one he wrote to Mum after the D Day landings, because you were not allowed to give away any information during the

war years, as it was all top secret. He was a Chief Petty Officer on H.M.S. Kimberly when they took Winston Churchill and the Commander-in-Chief of the Navy, I think it was Maitland, to Normandy a few days after the D-Day landings. In his letter he said he was so proud to carry the Commander-in-Chief's flag. During the war he had been torpedoed several times; one time he was rescued from the North Sea and was taken to a big house in Scotland that was used as a recovery centre. He couldn't swim but he had a life jacket and, with two or three others that couldn't swim, they threw a table overboard and clung to that until they were rescued.

Below: The dashing Jack Butler, Hazel's father.

Bill Sweet

Reg. I met Bill this morning at No 1 Crannacombe Cottages to talk about his early life. Bill where did you live before you came to Loddiswell?

Bill. I was born in Dawlish in 1930 and went to school there, the infants, then the junior school and then I went to the senior school, which was miles away from the town. Children out in the country were collected by 'bus but we had to walk. My first memories were playing at home in the kitchen or pottering around as we youngsters used to do. We lived in a Council house, which had a big garden, and we used to keep fowls, Mother was living then, that was a proper time, that was !

At school I enjoyed sport, football with my mates, us was devils then, that was when we were about thirteen or fourteen.

I liked school I always got on well with my lessons and liked the teachers. Sport was my main interest but I also liked history and geography, learning about places. I left school when I was 15 years old and went and did different jobs in the town. Back in they days I was an errand boy with a pushbike with a great big carrier up in the front. I used to go miles right up over the hills delivering groceries for customers that had been ordered. Dawlish is all

Bill's contentment with life radiates through his personality. A town boy who settled into a very rural area, which has given him great pleasure during his working life. He still enjoys its peace and beauty but relies on his trusty tractor for his regular visits to the village.

hills and people could not carry their groceries home in they days, there was no cars then. The shop had a van for delivering out in the country but otherwise I had to carry it on the bike.

I did this for a while and then I went into gardening at Sefton Hotel where women railway workers came to recuperate, the men stayed at the Bridge House next door. I then had to do my National Service from 1948 to 1950. I did my training at Oswestry in the Royal Artillery and then I was moved down to Aldershot and into the Royal Army Service Corp, from there I was sent across to Egypt. There was a big camp there in the desert with a high wire fence all the way around. I drove a ten-ton truck patrolling the outside, which was a long way round as it was a big camp. We didn't carry any guns 'cus the Arabs would pinch them, they would do that.

Several Egyptians worked in the camp and generally I enjoyed being there. I had some good mates and didn't want to leave them but I had to come home to be demobbed.

When I came out I dodged about a bit because someone else had taken my gardening job at the hotel. First I went on to a building job and then I found a job with the gas company and I was doing very well there. New mains would be put up through an avenue and I did the connections into the houses, that was a good job too.

I married Jean in about 1952, I had known her all my life, I knew her before I went into the Army and when I came out she had changed, she was a lovely girl and we got married. We decided then to make a move and leave Dawlish as work was getting scarce and we were stuck up in the Council estate, dead end place.

I saw an advertisement in the paper for a gardener/handyman so we came to Hazelwood to see about it. We liked it and the Hon. Mrs Peek drove us back to Plymouth Station to take the train back to Dawlish.

In those days Tom Soper worked here at Crannacombe, and others on the estate were Owen Ryder, Jim Thomas, Morley Dare, he lived up in the yard with his wife Kath and family. Jean and I lived at Weeke Moor where we brought up our family, Melvin, Garry, Peter, Tina and Maria. I didn't do much gardening, as there were two full time gardeners, Arthur Brimacombe and Stanley Manning. Mr Buscombe and his wife Lilian were with George Wakeham at Higher Hazelwood.

I worked with Tom Soper at Crannacombe Farm for Captain Peek where we had about 40 South Devon milking cows. We used a milking machine where the milk went through the jars direct to the churns but sometimes through a glass jar for recording. George Wakeham lived at Higher Hazelwood and looked after four or five cows up there and supplied the milk, cream and butter for Hazelwood House. I remember one day we had to go up and help him milk them by hand. George looked after the flock of sheep, which were sometimes entered in local shows and he also reared most of the calves from our herd.

We had a lovely lot of cows down here at Crannacombe and they grazed the fields all around here, that was a lovely job, I liked the cows. Most of them calved by themselves but sometimes we had one backwards and had to call the vet. If everything was all right I loved to see the calf struggle to get on its feet with Mother licking him all over.

We made thousands of bales of hay; all the staff from the estate joined in and helped stack the bales. Good days, that was, all working together. Capt. used to bring the kettle up for drinkings and we all sat around on the bales.

Reg. Did you ever drive a car?

Bill. When I was in the Army I drove a lorry but I never had a motorbike or car. I get around locally on my Ford 3000 tractor in all weathers and I can carry things in the link box. I was never really interested in driving and in the early days I couldn't afford it. Then the boys came along and they had their own transport and they often took us around.

My tractor is a little beauty and Capt. had it new. When it came Capt. said, "This is your tractor, Bill, don't let Tom knock it about" and I have still got it. I used a hedge trimmer on the Ford 4000, but I ploughed with a three-furrow plough on my tractor, it was better for that work. They were good days then, everybody wanted the food.

From where I came from 'twas like coming to another world. It was a new life for me, Jean and the boys liked it because it gave them freedom out here in the country. She missed the social life, going to the pictures and that, but with five children she was always busy.

We were able to go shopping in Kingsbridge on Wednesdays. Capt. arranged for the lorry to take all the estate staff and their wives to do their shopping. There was a green van but most times we went in the lorry which had a canvas top, 'course there were more people here in those days and there weren't many cars about then.

Below: South Devon cows at Crannacombe.

Reg. **Was the Hon Mrs Peek living at Hazelwood then?**

Bill. No she used to come to visit but she lived down at Flete, Holbeton then.

By the mid 1980s Tom Soper had retired and moved to Dartmouth; several others of the staff had left and part of the estate was put up for sale in about 1987. We moved in here No.1 Crannacombe Cottage and Capt. and Mrs Peek had Weeke Moor modernised and went to live there. I did odds and ends for Capt. and then I did some work for Col. Bye down at New Mill until they left in July this year 2003. I still go down there and help the new owners.

Reg **Do you follow the Loddiswell football team?**

Bill. I don't go to the matches but I go into the pub and have a little yap and hear all about it. When you come from Dawlish you never forget that team, so Dawlish is still in the back of my mind when I think about football.

I keep pretty well for a 73-year-old, 'twas all that running around after the cows and calves that

Above: "My tractor is a little beauty and Capt. had it new. When it came Capt. said, " This is your tractor, Bill, don't let Tom knock it about" and I have still got it."

kept me fit. I loved going out early in the morning as it was getting light bringing the cows in for milking. The dew was rising down over the fields and over the river Avon. I've had a good life and I still enjoy my days.

Below: Weeke Moor, where the family lived.

Bernard and Anne Kelly

*R*eg. *I am at Blackwell Parks, the home of Anne and Bernard Kelly. I have just come through the door where in 1891 the coachman, covered in snow, knocked and asked for help. He said the stagecoach was marooned in a six-foot snowdrift on the levels below here and could go no further. The passengers were scrambling over drifts trying to get to California Inn. He asked the farmer, Robert Popplestone, if he could leave his horses and stay the night. That was a long time ago, long before you knew the place Anne. When did you move here?*

Anne. We came here in 1971 from London but our early life was spent in Lancashire and Cheshire. I was in Swinton and Bernard was born further South at Hazel Grove in 1938. It was in the cotton mill country but during the war enemy planes on their way to bomb Liverpool Docks bombed the shops opposite. I remember going to school, it was St Augustine's Church School in Pendlebury.

It was a very old school with the toilets across the playground; it was very cold running across in winter. We lived in the house with my Grandma, the family were paper merchants

Anne and Bernard were born in Cotton Mill Country and Anne fell in love with Devon as a child when staying with relatives. Bernard and Anne both had stimulating and exciting jobs with the BBC, but thoughts often returned to the tranquillity and peace of rural Devon. They took the plunge in 1971 and slipped into the "Good Life" by buying Blackwell Parks, a move they have never regretted.

providing wrapping, greaseproof paper and bags for the shops. During the war period paper was in very short supply but was needed to wrap the small food rations. The paper was allocated to the shops, usually no more than half a ream to each shop. I remember my Mother used to sit at the kitchen table cutting up the squares of paper with a large kitchen knife. My Father was on haulage and then he was required during the war to do long distance haulage.

When I was at school we used to play netball, hopscotch and skipping. Another game we enjoyed was whipping tops, spinning them with a length of string. My next school was a private one at Prestwich. When the war came to an end my Father came back and revived the business obtaining a licence, which was necessary as paper was still in very short supply. During this time my brother was born but sadly he died at the age of four from leukaemia and a year or two later my sister was born. My Mother became very ill and I came down to Paignton with my baby sister to live with my Uncle and Aunt who was my Mother's sister. My Uncle was one of three brothers and he was able to get a farm at Yalberton. He found an old cider press and that was how the business of making Churchward's cider started. He was making 200,000 gallons at one time. They were very good as they had four children of their own and still took my sister and I.

I went to Paignton Secondary School when I was fourteen for one year and I always felt I would like to come back. I went home and we went to live in Hazel Grove, the town where my Father was born and that was where I met Bernard, when we were both 15. I got a job in local Government; that was the Urban District Council in those days. I was a junior clerk in the clerk's dept. They were very strict then about how one spoke to the public. It was drummed into us that the public were our employers. I attended evening classes and did shorthand and typing and then I went as secretary to the building inspector.

We were married in 1959 when I was just 21. I was then working as Secretary to the Planning Officer for North East Cheshire. Bernard passed his Higher National Diploma (HND) and obtained a job with the B.B.C. which meant moving to London. We had bought our own house when we got married but when we went down there they offered to find us a flat until we sold our own house. Someone from the B.B.C. asked what I did, when they knew I was a Secretary I was offered a job and that was how I joined the B.B.C.

*Reg. **Bernard, you seem to have known Anne for a very long time.***

Bernard. I was 15 when we first met and I still haven't escaped, I'm 65 this year.

*Reg. **You have left it too late!***

Bernard. I'm afraid so.

*Reg. **When you left school at 15 what did you do?***

Bernard. I did like a lot of other people did. In those days if you had a worker who did a good job his relatives would almost certainly get a job with the company and as I had a relative who worked for the Electricity Board. I was offered an apprenticeship with them in the North West of England. I did industrial metering to many of the large mills in the area. They took a lot of electricity, three phase supplies and they were

Above: New Lanark Woollen Mill.

quite complex to meter. I was in the department that used to build and maintain the equipment to supply the factories. It was more complicated than a normal house because the power factor has to be taken into account.

Many of the factories were built near a river to use water wheels or turbines; some changed over to steam power but the ones I was involved with were all electric. There is one mill, I believe the name is Style, which is now a working museum. It sticks in my memory today that when you go into one of these mills the noise was horrendous. When it was working the whole floors vibrated and bounced as the machines pounded away. Everyone there would lip-read, you couldn't speak to anybody because they wouldn't hear. I remember going in as a young man, 'course the place was full of young women and I could see them lip reading to each other, I hadn't a clue what they were saying, they would look at me and giggle, they were obviously saying something rude about me and they would all fall about laughing. The activity was tremendous, one woman would be looking after six machines, they really did work hard.

When I was with the Electricity Board they provided day release on one day a week. I was able to obtain a National Certificate and having got that I saw an advert in the newspaper for people suitable to become engineers in the B.B.C. I think it was about the time B.B.C. 2 was starting up. I went to the interview and was told you will have a better chance when you've got your HND in electronics. If you come then you will be considered, so that's what I did. The problem was I could not take an HND in electronics with the Electricity Board.

I changed my job to a firm called Avro which was a company about three miles from where I lived. My Father worked there during the war, they built the Lancaster bomber and also the Vulcan. Surprisingly I worked on the Blue Steel missile, which is a nuclear weapon, this was at the time of the Cold War. It was carried by the Vulcan bomber and I worked in the design department as a draughtsman mainly on the autopilot. As this was a vital job it was considered as my National Service before that service was discontinued.

I was able to get my HND and reapplied to the B.B.C., and to my amazement they employed me. Needless to say most of their jobs were in London so I began on outside broadcasts and that was extremely interesting. It allowed me to go to Wimbledon each year, the Grand National, the Queen's Enclosure at Ascot, to Buckingham Palace to meet the Queen when she did her Christmas broadcast, to Downing Street and meet different Prime Ministers, including Harold

Below: Bernard Kelly in the BBC television van of outside broadcasts in the 1960s.

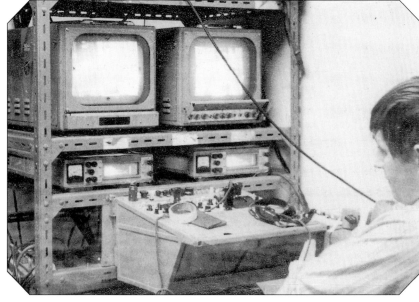

Wilson. I used to go to political conferences, in fact I travelled anywhere the B.B.C. sent me. Outside broadcasts covered everything, which was not on B.B.C. premises. If there was a football match or golf tournament we were there.

Reg. *How do they manage to connect up all those hundreds of cables correctly?*

Bernard. I had the esteemed position of being an engineer with the camera crew. We employed what we call rigger drivers to do that, they used to take all the equipment there and connect it up. When I turned up with the television crew we would do the programme and then leave them to clear up.

Anne. On arrival in London I attended an interview for a job in the Planning Office at the B.B.C. in Outside Broadcasting, which was at the Palace of Art, near Wembley Stadium. During the interview I said my husband is based there and she said "Oh, we can't have you both in the same department!" they were very strict on that. Next day she phoned to say there was a job in the transport department and I could work there as a clerk. I was doing time sheets and I had never seen one before!

I was very lucky because the senior transport officer and his assistant took me under their wings. The officer was pleased that I, as a clerk, was a qualified shorthand typist, which he never had before.

Then they decided to merge outside broadcasting transport and Television Transport which was at Fulham, and I was lucky that I was in the right place at the right time. I went there in charge of the office; there were six clerks and when they were doing filming we had to arrange transport. I remember *Dr Finley's Casebook* when we were responsible for arranging transport for wardrobe and props to Scotland. We arranged the rota for the drivers, they did not have taco graphs in those days they had to fill in their own log sheets.

I was there for about six years and

then moved into Television Centre and the programme planning department, working with directors and controllers as an administration assistant, a bit like personnel really. They were then making another unit looking after all the technical staff at Television Centre, which was about 2000 people. By then the News programmes had been brought in from Alexandra Palace, they built a special extension for them. I was then in charge of the administration of all the technical staff in the Television Centre. I was there for two years and then we came down here to Devon in 1971.

Bernard. Much as I liked my job in London I could not see myself settling down there. We were really enamoured with the South Hams, partly because Anne's Uncle lived here and we used to come down to stay.

One day we saw an old farm house, it sounds crazy, but somebody had bought it and started to do 'bed and breakfast' there. We thought if we could live in this beautiful area and earn a modest income that would be great, it set us thinking. I thought if I could get a transfer to Plymouth we could live down here. It took me two or three years to get a transfer but eventually colour television was threatening to come down here. They were desperate to have at least one person conversant with colour television and as I had worked on colour television since it's introduction I applied and got the job in Plymouth.

Anne. If I could have transferred down here I wouldn't have looked to do 'bed and breakfast' but there was nothing suitable for me. We then looked around for a house where bed and breakfast could be done. The farm we had seen earlier was Longcombe Farm and not far from Yalberton my Uncle's home.

Reg. *That was not far from William of Orange's first Parliament House!*

Anne. I know the cottage, my cousin lives next door to it. The lady, Mrs Jury lived there and she looked after my baby sister when we came down as children. There is a moulding on the ceiling above the table where the Parliament sat.

Blackwell Parks is the first house we came to see

Above: "Blackwell Parks is the first house we came to see and we fell in love with it. It needed a lot of renovation, but we loved the place and that was it."

and we fell in love with it. It needed a lot of renovation, but we loved the place and that was it. That was 32 years ago and we have no regrets on opting for the "Good Life.".

Reg. *Where does your daughter's interest in horses come from?*

Anne. My Grandfather was a horse breaker and was very fond of his own horses. When they were commandeered in the First World War he went with them to see they were well cared for. My daughter who was born here loves horses too and has her own carriage teams, which have been hired for weddings. She also enjoys driving and riding which she has done since she was four year old. She drives as a pair or singly.

The bed and breakfast business eventually took over and Bernard gave up his job in 1978 to help run the business.

Right: Elsa Kelly, aged 16, driving with her tutor Mr Foland acting as her groom at Smith Lawn, Windsor Great Park in 1990 when she won second prize.

Betty Sampson

Reg. When interviewing my wife, Betty Sampson, at our home at Lilwell, Loddiswell my first comment was, "You were not born in Loddiswell Parish?"

Betty. No. I was born at West Hartley Farm, Blackawton in 1924. Our farmhouse was large and rambling, with a dairy, larger than the kitchen, which faced north and always seemed freezing cold. The kitchen opened into a long alleyway leading to the pump house and the milk house. Further along was the toilet with a long wooden bench seat for two!! The milk was brought into the milk house each morning and evening and poured into a large steel holding bowl on the top of the separator. One of the men would turn the handle setting the separator in motion to extract the cream into one pan and the skimmed milk into a large bucket. This milk was fed to the calves in the adjoining houses and if any milk remained it was fed to the pigs.

My Father was in a tenanted farm of a 160 acres and as there were no cottages attached to the farm, the three farm workers, and a girl who helped my Mother, lived in and made up the household.

Reg. This appears to be a large workforce compared to today?

Betty has vividly described her early life as if it was yesterday, but time has intervened and relegated it to an era of long ago. She is full of ideas, most of which are progressive and exciting.
If only the rest of us could keep up!

Betty. This was in the late twenties and early thirties before tractors were in use on the farms so horses provided the power. The farm grew many acres of corn, as well as root crops for the sheep and milking cows, and one man was employed as the head horse-man.

He usually rose at six, cleaned, fed and watered his horses before breakfast at 7.45 am. The other two men and my Father did the milking, separating, feeding the calves and other livestock before breakfast. I can still remember, however, a huge bowl of cream was always left in the dairy so the men helped themselves to a large slice of bread from a four pound loaf, spread with cream, before starting work.

The main breakfast was fried eggs, bacon, fried-mashed potatoes, liver or hogs pudding too, if a pig had been recently killed. Our water for the house was carried from the pump house and the livestock water taken from a trough in the yard.

Reg. Were the men employed from the local parish?

Betty. I am not sure, but I remember we had one family from Ireland, William, Charley and Morton. William came first and, after a few months, his brother Charley agreed to come. My Father was not impressed when he met him at Totnes station as he looked a mere boy. On

Above: Betty and elder sister, Joan with Mother and Father and Uncle Tom Sherriff, on the right, at West Hartley Farm, Blackawton. 1929

asking him his age he said, "Sixteen Sir." It later transpired he was only thirteen but brother Charley had last minute reservations about coming, so Morton quickly took his place. Charley eventually agreed to come for a short while before moving on to another farm.

Morton was a good worker and my sister and I, who were small children then, enjoyed his company. His Irish sayings frequently puzzled us especially, "I be after fur going," when asked if he had done a job. We had many hair-raising adventures with him and it is not surprising that, later in his working life he became a steeplejack!

Reg. Your Mother had a large family to feed?

Betty. Yes, not only did she bake and cook for all the men, carry the water from the pump house and heat it in large boilers over the open hearth, but filled and trimmed the oil lamps every day. After the cream had been scalded and cooled, it was made into butter every other day. She also kept several hundred hens to supply her weekly customers at Dartmouth Market.

The strict regime of the household never altered. Monday was washday; the copper boiler was filled and lit by seven in the morning, and the washing took up most of the day in the pump house. Each batch of clothes was boiled in the copper boiler and, after rinsing in cold water, was put through the hand operated mangle to extract the surplus water. Tuesday was baking day and Wednesday cleaning. My sister and I really enjoyed helping with some

jobs, like the annual carpet cleaning. Each day the carpet cleaning involved a dustpan and brush or a long-handled cleaner which was pushed over the carpet to collect the dust, it usually created more dust than it collected. In the Spring on a really fine day my Mother would decide to spring-clean the carpet. It was folded up and taken in the wheelbarrow to the grass field in front of the house, laid out on the grass and by using the old wicker beaters we'd flog it with all the strength we could muster, we would see who could raise the largest cloud of dust. After five minutes, and in sheer exhaustion we would collapse on the carpet in the middle of the field. The pleasure of lying there with the open sky and the sun pouring down was sheer joy!

On Thursday preparations were made for Dartmouth pannier market, plucking chickens and hens, weighing up the butter and cream and preparing vegetables in season. Friday was market day. My Father loaded the horse and cart with the produce, sometimes up to 100 dozen eggs, packed in 15 dozen boxes, and took them to the top of the lane where Mother caught the bus. The bus had a metal rail around the top with a ladder at the back to climb up with all the produce. The goods were secured to the rail and when she arrived at Dartmouth market a kindly retired policeman was always waiting for my Mother to help her unload.

Market day was a business day, serving the regular customers, ordering poultry and calf food for the next month and paying for the last. It gave her an opportunity to meet the neighbours and have a social chat during the lunchtime. The produce was usually sold by early afternoon and a fishmonger, who had his barrel of fish at the entrance to the market, always came and offered Mother his surplus fish. Sometimes there would be six or seven pounds for which he charged her one shilling and six pence (three and a half pence) so it was always fish for tea on Fridays, usually whiting.

The weekly ten-pound joint of beef was collected, and the monthly grocery order was passed into Cundells for delivery to the farm during the following week. We provided our own lamb on the farm (or usually mutton in those days) and pork; a pig was killed every ten weeks and cured. In those days pigs were twice the size and twice as fat as they are today and we all ate home-cured fat bacon. Hogs puddings were made and simmered in the copper boiler; hams and shoulders were cured and hung to smoke in the hearth chimney.

Reg. What happened at the weekends?

Betty. Saturday was another cooking day, and bath night for the whole household. Water was heated and carried to a large metal bath on the back landing for the women and children. The men had their's in the pump house, and all the clothes and bedding was changed for Monday's washday.

Sunday was a welcome relief for man and beast; that is, after feeding and watering all the stock. Not much rest for Mother however, she would set off for church at 10.30 am. My sister Joan and I had to accompany her most Sundays but every time I went the service dragged on and often it was 1.30 pm. before we arrived home. Occasionally my Father could be persuaded that he needed us to move some sheep; what a joy it was to set off with the dogs and a pet lamb that always joined us for a Sunday morning walk.

Our vicar, the Rev Charnell, was very elderly and forgetful. We sat in church on several occasions waiting for him to come, and I remember my

Below: West Hartley Farm.

Mother was often delegated to go and find him in order to take the service. On one occasion he was just getting out of the bath, and was going to catch the bus to Dartmouth, thinking it was Saturday!

With several men in our household, all doing heavy and often dirty work, their clothes needed major repairs. In the late twenties and early thirties the workhouse at Totnes took disabled and destitute men and women and each autumn a disabled man called Vivian was collected by my Father from the workhouse. He spent several months with us, mending shirts, trousers, breeches, sheets and any other sewing that was necessary. There was a large treadle sewing machine on the back landing where he worked in the winter months, eating and sleeping with us until he returned to the workhouse in the spring.

Reg. How did you spend the long dark evenings?

Betty. We only had oil lamps and candles for lighting so if we wanted to read we would sit around the table near the oil lamp. We also played cards or board games at the table; darts and rings provided entertainment for the more energetic. I remember when my Father in the early thirties bought our first wireless set; we sat in awe around it and marvelled that this elevated voice was speaking directly to us in our own kitchen. There were remarks from the farm workers like, "Cau blimey," and "Av'e niver he'rd nor't like't." but perhaps this was one of our first steps into a more sophisticated way of life.

The wireless was powered by a heavy glass accumulator, which stored the electricity. It was charged up at the nearest garage in Dartmouth once a fortnight, so listening time was limited; otherwise the accumulator would run down too soon.

Reg. Your early school days were at Blackawton?

Betty. The school at Blackawton was about a mile from the farm. The parish covered a wide rural area and a high proportion of the children attending the school were from farming backgrounds. My sister and I often met other children at Langstone Cross, the Wakehams,

Haymans, Tozers, Shillabeers, and Lethbridges.

In the summertime we would take our hoops to school, the boys had metal ones and the girls wooden hoops. The last half-mile to school was downhill and we would race at breakneck speed down the hill. In those days the only motorised vehicle using the road was Mr Cutmore, the butcher, who went to Dartmouth market on Tuesdays and Fridays and on those days we always listened to hear if his van had started coming up the steep hill out of Blackawton before we set off.

The pressures in my early school days were not too demanding. Our Infant Teacher, Miss Bond was kind and a great favourite with the children. The country children all took packed lunches, which were quickly eaten so that we had an hour's freedom to explore outside the school playground.

The most vivid memory was going to the ruins of Oldstone Mansion and terrifying each other with ghost stories of the bride that was drowned in the lake. Sometimes we visited the tunnel leading to the hermit's cave on the edge of the wood and collected the empty snail shells, which were said to be from his main diet. The middle school was uneventful but the senior class under the headmaster, Mr Blight, was ruled with a rod of iron. I remember even small children, if they were late, being sent to him and having the cane. One family who lived over two miles from the school usually managed to arrive as the bell was ringing, but sometimes they couldn't make it. On their late arrival they always had the cane and it was no excuse that they had to milk three cows each before starting for school.

My sister and I were saved the wrath of the headmaster's class as, when she was eleven years old, my sister went to Twyford School at Kingsbridge and I followed two years later. My sister was a boarder, but when I went there farming was in a financially depressed state so we became day-girls. We stayed with my Father's parents, John and Lizzie Walke during the week. They had retired to Kingsbridge, and then, after school on Fridays, we caught the train to Loddiswell to stay with my Mother's parents,

William and Selina Elliott. They lived at Tyepitte House where they had retired from the Baker's shop.

We always looked forward to the weekends. My Grandfather loved outside activities and we enjoyed many long walks with him to Hatch bridge, New Mill, up the river to Topsham and back through Reads or Silveridge Lane. After attending Church on Sunday morning it was usually a short walk.

The Rev. George Bliss filled the pulpit, not only with his personality but his dynamic and eloquent sermons, his recurring phrase, "let me reiterate," will never be forgotten by all who knew him. A far cry from Mr Charnell's sleepy monologue at Blackawton when some of the hardworking community welcomed and enjoyed a quite doze through his long sermon.

I enjoyed my childhood when we made our own amusements and I loved helping with the animals, and walking in the countryside.

I do not remember my Mother observing the social etiquettes that my Grandmother Walke often talked about. In the early 20th century Grandma Walke moved from Hazelwood Farm with the younger boys of her family to Butterford, North Huish. The farmhouse was huge with a large ballroom and afternoon tea parties were very much in fashion. When having tea at the Manor the hostess rang a little silver bell and the maid appeared in her white lace apron and frilly cap, and served tea to the guests.

My Grandmother was impressed and when she returned home she related this to Bessie who helped in the house. Bessie said, "But we could do that here!" so the smart apron and cap were made and at the next tea party the little bell was placed near Grandma which she duly rang when the time arrived. Bessie did not appear even after the third time the bell was rung and Grandma had to go to the kitchen where Bessie was oblivious to the ringing bell. Bessie hastily collected herself and as she hurried into the sitting room, across the polished floor, she tripped over the mat and the whole tray came crashing to the floor!

*Reg. **What year did you leave the farm?***

136

Betty. My Father became ill in 1939 and, after a series of operations, died of pneumonia in September of that year. We were required to vacate the farm by the following March. My Father had been self-employed so my Mother could not receive a widow's pension. He had voluntarily joined a private Government Pension Scheme two years earlier but as only a hundred and two weekly payments had been made, and the Government required a hundred and four to be eligible, they would not grant her a widow's pension.

In order to make a living she decided to find a house and a couple of fields that could be rented and she would continue with the poultry side of the business. I think she favoured returning to the Kingsbridge area as she was born in Loddiswell and remembered her teenage years at the shop. She often talked about her trips delivering bread with her brother William to outlying farms in the area, and when the Monks came to Wood Barton in 1902 they had to deliver bread twice weekly to the Monastery before the kitchens were built there. They journeyed down Silveridge Lane and over the river up to Wood Barton where the Monks always insisted they had a meal of bread and cheese with wine before returning home.

My Grandfather knew Lilwell Cottage was empty and Mrs Conran, of the Woolston House Estate, agreed my Mother could rent the cottage. At that time Mr L R Sampson took on Woolston Farm and agreed to letting her two fields; little did I realise he would be my future Father-in-law!

In 1940 we came to Lilwell Cottage, without any electricity, an outside loo and the water at the bottom of the garden! My sister who was training to be a kindergarten teacher, had to leave her training and get a job, but with the outbreak of war she was called into the Forces the following year. My Mother continued going to Dartmouth market, hiring a taxi to take her each week. I helped her look after the poultry and maintain our small-holding.

U-boats were sinking our shipping in the North Atlantic in 1941 and this greatly reduced our food supplies so we had to boil two or three hundredweights of potatoes daily to make up the poultry rations.

Pure breeding stock had been seriously depleted and as all our hens were pure bred Rhode Island Reds, White Wyndotte and Light Sussex we applied to enter the Ministry of Agriculture and Fisheries (MAFF) breeding scheme. This entitled us to extra food rations to maintain healthy stock. Our eggs were sold to approved hatcheries, Sterlings at Okehampton, Farmers at Ottery-St-Mary and any surplus to Trotts at South Brent. The delivery of hatching eggs was quite difficult, as they often had to be sent on the train from Loddiswell Station. The weekly trip to Dartmouth then ceased.

In 1944 my cousin Bert Elliott was home on leave from the RAF and he offered to find a car for me. He was a motor mechanic before joining up and was able to locate a 1939 Ford Popular car.

Reg. I remember teaching you to drive!

Betty. Yes, that was fun. Learning to drive was easy in those days; there were few cars on the road owing to the petrol restrictions and providing you avoided the army convoys all was well. I was then able to deliver the eggs to Okehampton and Ottery-St-Mary by car on a weekly basis.

As petrol was not allowed to be used for social

Below: Accredited breeding flock. Rhode Island Reds and Light Sussex hens. 1952

events we often cycled to dances at Modbury and Kingsbridge with a group of friends and enjoyed the journey. One night we were returning from a dance at Modbury and the lights of my bicycle failed. As I reached a slight incline a policeman stepped out in front of me and shouted, "Halt" Excuses were of no avail and in the Plymouth Times the following week the headlines read, "Loddiswell girl fined for riding a bicycle after dark without lights."

It seems incredible now that such a petty crime should reach the headlines but news was often in short supply as all military activities or bomb damage was censored.

During and after the war Miss Christian Michell wrote and produced pantomimes and plays,

Below: Carnival time, Introduction of Free Health and Dental Service for all. 1948 "I Pullum" Left to Right: Henry Martin, Reg Sampson (dentist). Herbert Harvey (patient). Florence Todd (nurse). In the waiting room. Bill Eversfield, Eva Kernick, Betty Sampson.

which ran for three nights in the village before going to outside venues. Although we often lost our lines during rehearsals it always seemed to go well on the night. It was at this time the village held an annual carnival.

Individuals throughout the war years did a considerable amount of voluntary work to help the War Effort, the Home Guard, Women's Voluntary Service, Air Raid Wardens, Special Police Force, Billeting Officers and Fire Fighters. The Government appealed to everyone to save money and to contribute each week to the horrendous cost of the war. Savings groups were set up in each area. Miss Margaret Common organised Loddiswell's saving group at the school. Each Savings Certificate cost fifteen shillings, (75p) which was quite a lot of money in those days as the average man's weekly wage was about 32 shillings and six pence (£1·62 in present currency). In order to get people to save small amounts, savings stamp books were issued so people could contribute a little each week and when enough stamps were collected they

could be exchanged by the collector for a certificate. Collectors were required to do weekly rounds and I did the north end of the parish on my bicycle, starting at Topsham Bridge and on to Hazelwood, Coldharbour, Wizaller, Chillaton, Stanton and Woolston.

Our marrying in 1947 was no great surprise. We had known each other for a few years; you were kind and often rather serious, maybe I was a little more wayward but our life together has been great. When we married we were able to rent 50 acres of Alleron Farm and your Father let us rent 40 acres of Woolston where we kept milking cows and cattle.

The most profitable section of the farm was the poultry business and we decided to extend it. Within the next three years our hen flock had increased to 2,500 breeding hens on controlled range. All the slatted floored houses and rearing arks were made on the farm.

The demand for food was very critical in the forties and early fifties and the demand for day old chicks exceeded the supply. In 1950 we decided to start hatching some of our own eggs, but as we did not have electricity we were required to pay for the line to be brought from Woolston Farm. When this was completed the incubator house was built and a 6000 egg size Secura incubator installed, this was followed by a 12,000 size Stephens. This enabled us to hatch approximately 4,000 chicks a week, many of which were collected from the farm or delivered locally.

A warm and draught-free environment is essential in the first few weeks of the chick's life so, to meet the demand for four-week-old chicks, we extended our brooding capacity. You built a 120 ft. long brooder house divided into twelve compartments, each holding 300 chicks, reared under electric canopy brooders. At four weeks old the chicks were nearly feathered and did not require heat so they could be dispatched to our customers.

In the early sixties larger orders were being placed and customers who had ordered 500 or 1000 pullet chicks when we started then wanted 5000. This would require a large expansion programme for us and with tighter

Above: Rearing chicken in the brooder house. 1957

profit margins it did not seem a prudent venture. We had also acquired Woolston and Stanton farms so the poultry business was run down and then discontinued.

*Reg. **What about the family?***

Betty. Yes, the family occupied a considerable amount of my time in the sixties. My Mother was becoming frail after a major operation and it was then Doris Sharland came to help me two mornings a week. Doris was a great help and support to all the family and she continued helping me for the next 35 years until our retirement in 1997.

We became involved in a farm requisite Buying Group (Avon Farmers Ltd) whose offices were here at Lilwell for the next three years before moving to Kingsbridge. It was after this period I started hobby wine making which eventually led to planting 60 vines in the garden in 1972.

*Reg. **Who's idea was it to plant a vineyard?***

Betty. I can't say that I was really responsible. Our son John had come home on the farm by then and started looking for diversifications. We had redundant poultry and pig buildings here, which could be converted, so in 1977 we planted our first four acres, eventually extending to 10 acres of vines. So started one of the most challenging and enjoyable experiences of my life.

Reg Sampson

My primary school education began in 1930 and I still remember the first day. My Mother had walked with me the three quarters of a mile up across the path fields to the school where there were more children than I had ever seen. We entered a classroom and met an enormous lady with a long flowing navy blue skirt who said a few words to my Mother. I learned that she was to be my teacher; she grabbed me by the hand and I quickly looked for Mother, she was gone.

Schooling soon fell into a pleasant pattern of lessons and holidays. In the wintertime two boys from the top class were delegated to stoke up the large round tortoise stoves to heat the classrooms. Coke had to be brought in and the red-hot clinkers, which had melted together, had to be removed. A poker was used to loosen them and lever them out of the little door at the bottom. We found a red-hot poker was the ideal tool for burning holes in the wooden floor when no one was looking.

The real bliss was walking home from school in the summer sunshine and listening to the clatter of the mowing machine, the chorus of crickets and the smell of new mown hay. With my head in the clouds it is not surprising that I invariably

Reg's life story covers many different aspects; school days at Loddiswell, Kingsbridge Grammar School, the exploits of the Home Guard and his farming life, coupled with many local and regional public commitments. During the years his philosophy has been, " Never say no, think how you are going to do it afterwards!"

forgot to bring home Father's two ounces of loose cut plug tobacco on Thursdays and had to hurry back to the village before the shop closed. It was my job on Saturday mornings to ride the pony, with a square market basket on my arm, to the butcher's shop for the Saturday joint. I tied the pony to the railings on the Bank at Loddiswell and used the steps to remount with the heavy basket. The usual order was for 10 lbs of brisket. Butcher Walke would cut off a piece, put it on the scales and contemplate, "'Tis 12 lbs, is that all right?" Well who was I to argue!

The baker, on his country rounds would call at the farm on Tuesdays and Saturdays, and the grocer from Worlds Stores, Kingsbridge would call in on Wednesdays, once a month. He would deliver all that was needed and take the order for the next month's delivery, flour, sugar, tea, salt, yeast, Puritan soap and so on. Persil soap powder was needed to facilitate the boiling and scrubbing of all the clothes in the large copper in the wash-house.

This copper was also used to scald the large pans of milk to produce clotted cream each morning. They were taken to the dairy where they were cooled and next morning the cream was skimmed off ready to be taken to

Loddiswell Butts to meet W J Guests milk lorry for Addison's Cafe in Torquay. Some milk went through the separator for butter making and the remaining skimmed and separated milk was used to rear the calves and piglets.

On the farm we all had our own jobs to do. I was responsible for feeding the two-dozen hens, collecting the eggs and taking the skimmed milk to the calves. They would be out to grass in the springtime and when they heard the pails rattling would come charging across the meadow in an effort to be the first to be fed. Some great big babies would not drink unless they could suck one's finger under the milk.

Visits to Uncle and Aunt's were not always holidays either. Uncle Jack Heathman at Marridge Farm would say, "Auntie is cooking a good dinner today so we will go up and move the sheep fences in the turnips, then after dinner you will be able to cut the lawn". That seemed to be a good idea until one discovered the grass was 6 inches high and the mower had to be pushed.

I remember, in the early 1930s, we had a horse very ill with colic. I had probably allowed him to drink too much cold water when he came in from the fieldwork steaming hot. We hastily sent for 'Doctor' Billy Stear, the vet at Aveton Gifford who usually came on his motorbike and sidecar, but this time he arrived in a new Austin 7 with George Steer of Yabbacombe as a passenger. 'Tiger' had his medicine and, while we waited for the horse's recovery, George Shepherd

Below: South Devon cows in the yard at Higher Yanston, Loddiswell. 1936

invited the company to sample his newly barrelled cider. The cellar was full of casks and everyone enjoyed the comparison between one cask and the next. The time came when we stumbled across the yard to the stable and 'Tiger' was much better. We lit the way to Doctor Billy's car with our Hurricane lanterns while he explicitly explained the wonders of a modern car. He squeezed in, with George in the passenger seat and away with a flourish of hand waving.

We hadn't gone far up the yard when we heard a crash; Doctor Billy had turned the corner rather carelessly and landed the car on its side. We hurried back and I held up the lantern as Father reached up on top to open the door and look in. There was the shining top of Doctor Billy's head, he was saying, "Come on George, do 'e get out," to which George replied, "I can't, y'um sitting on me. Cor dun'e let 'en catch on fire. Cor. dun'e let 'en!"

Sunday was a day of rest or so we were told. Of course the cows had to be milked and the livestock fed and this would take about three hours mornings and afternoons. Our family would regularly attend the morning service at eleven o'clock and listen to the expositions of the Rev. George Bliss during his half hour sermon. He seemed to be very conversant with the great theologians and in case we did not hear the first time would often repeat a few sentences prefixed by 'Let me reiterate'. We were careful not to cough to attract attention from the pulpit as one of my friends was reprimanded in the middle of a sermon for playing with his handkerchief. He and his family refused to come to Loddiswell church again after being so publicly affronted.

Bible Study with Mrs Bliss at Sunday school in the afternoons was rather more relaxing, before returning home to do the essential farm work. On many Sunday evenings I would accompany my Mother to the Wesleyan Chapel at Aveton Gifford, about a mile and a half away, and then walk home again through the rain, or under a beautifully star-lit sky. It cannot be said that my Mother neglected any of her duties in pointing me in the way I should go and for this I am extremely grateful.

Our near neighbours, the Shepherds at Lower Yanston, occasionally invited us on a Sunday evening, which we youngsters rather enjoyed because, after listening to the Rev Dick Shepherd of St. Martin's in the Field in London on the old wireless, we could go for walks over the farm. When we returned Florrie, who helped in the house, would be preparing supper in the kitchen and we loved to listen to her newest records on her gramophone. I think these secular songs on a Sunday rather disturbed her conscience so, before taking supper to the front room she would always end with a hymn 'For ever with the Lord, Amen, so let it be'.

Jim Lethbridge worked on our farm for many years doing the general farm work, driving horses, building hay and corn ricks, hoeing the root crops, in fact, turning his hand to anything that had to be done. Morning and noon he would make his way to the cellar to fill his keg with cider to quench his thirst during the day.

Each morning Jim would bring the dozen South Devon cows into the yard and I was often awakened by Jim's rusty voice on a rainy morning as he burst into his favourite song.

'I was walking through the churchyard in the city when I met a beggar old and grey, with his arms outstretched he asked the folks for pity, and it made me sad to hear him say,
"Oh, I wonder, yes I wonder, will the angels way up yonder, will the angels play their harps for me?
For a million miles I've travelled and a million sights I've seen and I'm ready for the glory soon to be.
Oh, I wonder, yes I wonder will the angels play their harps for me."

Mother felt this song was very unsuitable for us youngsters and we were forbidden to sing it.

In 1936 I went to the Kingsbridge Grammar School and each day it was necessary to walk the two miles to Loddiswell Station to catch the steam train. School took up six days of the week with football or cricket on Wednesday and Saturday afternoons. When I was not listed for

Above: Threshing at Higher Yanston. 1936

football or cricket I would walk the four miles back home where there was always work to do. The chance of a lift was remote although sometimes it was possible to hold on to the back of Hyne's stone lorry slowly labouring up Coombe Royal Hill. It was important, however, to let go at the top before it gathered speed or we would suffer the same fate as one of our number who let go rather late and fell flat on his face.

Saturday afternoon at home gave an opportunity to do my 'prep' early whilst the aroma of Mother's batch of dough cakes filled the kitchen.

The ricks of corn were threshed during the winter months and after a lot of preparation we would listen to hear the traction engine and thresher coming down the lane. It was quite a steep pull up into Sugar Park and sometimes the thresher had to be winched into place. Half a ton of coal and a cart with a cask of water would be brought ready for next morning. About five o'clock next morning Jack Baker and his man would light up and then come in for breakfast. We had to finish the milking and turn out the cows and be ready at eight o'clock with the neighbours who had come to help. In due course we would return to help them.

By spring the store cattle, to which we had carried bundles of hay through the winter, were ready for the Spring Store Sale at Kingsbridge. About four of us would drive them along the by-roads to avoid the few lorries and cars, which could frighten them. Along Clarks Barn Road,

Above: Family group at Woolston. 1943. Left to Right: Mother, Reg, Sybil, Leslie and Father.

Hatch Bridge, Leigh Cross and Darky Lane into Kingsbridge. The Market by this time would be full of cattle and we had to wait until ours were sold. Another hour would be spent grouping them with others that the buyers had bought and then about a dozen of us would drive them to the station yard where they would be loaded into railway trucks.

I remember on one occasion Father said "Fourteen pounds a head for good two and a half year old steers is not enough, that won't pay the rent. We must drive them home." In those days the farm rent was by far the largest expense on most farms.

Many farms supplemented their income in the 1930s by taking in visitors and our farm was no exception. I was interested in the cars they drove. One family came regularly in a 'Bean' and another in a large 'Lagonda' with a folding roof. Our neighbour, Mr. George Shepherd had an open top 'Overland' but this was being outclassed by these visitors from the Cities.

In 1938 my brother Leslie and I were invited to spend a week in London with one of these families. I remember the combine harvesters being hauled by caterpillar tractors as we crossed Salisbury Plain and thought what a saving of time and effort could be made by using these machines.

We stayed with Mr. Hunt and his family, who, with his brother, had a packaging factory in North London employing 1,000 girls and 50 men. The half-ton rolls of card or paper were brought to the factory by barge as the canal flowed alongside. Boxes and cartons were made for soap powders, cheeses and a number of other products. I was thirteen years old and was very interested in the photographic department where their son, Gordon was an apprentice. He was about 17 years old.

Mr. Hunt accompanied us the first day around London advising us to eat at Lyons or ABC Cafe's and travel mainly by tube. In the afternoon we went to Radio Olympia and there we had our first experience of seeing television. The screens were about twelve inches square with black and white pictures, showing mainly Music Hall acts. I particularly remember Will Fife and Harry Lauder in their kilts, joking and singing in their Scottish brogue. My brother and I saw more of the historic places and museums in one week than many Londoners, in those days, would have seen in a lifetime.

The experience made me begin to think about the routine work at home and I began to realise that 80 per cent of the time on the farm was being spent on unprofitable work, paring hedges, cutting weed, re-building broken hedges and fences, but at that stage I could not see a way round it. Labour was modestly cheap and the necessary machines had not been invented. I shall always treasure the memories of Kingsbridge Grammar School and the academic scramble between Ken Stone, Bill Mitchell, Owen Winzer and myself. The physical cost of this rivalry was the burden of books needed for prep to be carried to the Kingsbridge Station and from Loddiswell Station, two miles to our farm.

My scholastic life came to an abrupt end in 1940 because war had recently been declared and we were then farming 240 acres. The only staff left on the farm was my older brother and my ageing father and the War Agricultural Committee demanded that a 180 acres must be ploughed to grow wheat and barley and five acres of potatoes. The penalty for not complying could be eviction and the committee would come in and do the work. This happened to a farmer in an adjoining parish.

My brother and I, with our teams of six horses, did all the ploughing, cultivating and harvesting until 1942 when we were able to buy our first Fordson tractor. We still had the twenty-five cows to milk each day, the hay and corn ricks to build and thatch. There was no time to spare and food was desperately short as shipping convoys from the USA were being attacked, and many of them sunk by U boats.

I was required to register for Military Service as I reached the age of 17 in 1942 and to the question, "What service would you like to be in?" I replied, "RAF." Next question, "In what capacity?" Reply, "Pilot or Navigator." A week or two later I was told that the War Agricultural Committee would not release me from a Reserved Occupation as there was no one to take my place and I was promptly pushed into the Home Guard!

Home Guard drills, lectures and manoeuvres usually took place at weekends and on one occasion we were challenged by the marine commandos to a mock invasion exercise. One of the purposes of the Home Guard was to create organised resistance and delay the enemy until reinforcements could be brought in. The obvious position where this may be possible was at Loddiswell Bridge. Entrenchments had been prepared in Rake orchard on the east side of the bridge and in the brake up over on the west side giving 120 degrees cover of the bridge.

Along the sides of the road for a hundred yards on the Loddiswell side were two-inch perforated pipes linked to a fuel tank near the west-side entrenchment. In the event of an invasion the intention was to ignite the roadway in the path of an advancing column, while the bridge was covered by two Lewis guns and anti-tank cup-dischargers. Corporal Percy Baker would take his squad to the Rake side and I, who by that time was a Lance-corporal and a qualified Lewis Gunner, took my squad of eight men to the Loddiswell side.

On the Sunday when the Marines were attacking we took up our positions by the bridge. I had three men on the Lewis gun, two with cup-dischargers for lobbing anti-tank

Below: There were very few trees near Loddiswell Bridge in those days.

Above: Friesian cows coming in for milking at Stanton Farm. 1968

grenades and reserves with standard 303 rifles. I was equipped with a Sten, close-combat automatic.

The marines were coming from the Torcross training area but we were ready for them. They came, however, through Halwell and Gara Bridge and into the village from the north, capturing the part of our platoon, which was deployed in the village. My father, who had the strange title of Chairman of the Invasion Committee, saw them approaching HQ in Wyselands, picked up all the vital papers and left by the back door. Being in civvies he was not seen, but Mrs Selina Yabsley saw a Marine tying up one of our men in the village square and attacked him with her broom. We had, however, to admit defeat.

One night when we were on duty we were alerted that a large group of marine commandos had been landed on Slapton Sands and were marching in the direction of Kingsbridge. It seemed a good opportunity to teach them a lesson as we were in full kit and ready to go. We quickly drove to Frogmore picking up some reinforcements on the way and took up positions in the gardens each side of the road. The Marines marched right into the ambush and were forced to concede that they could have been annihilated. The element of surprise with which they had overrun Loddiswell a few weeks before had been turned on them and I believe the Home Guard thereafter was considered with more respect.

In early April 1944 convoys of U.S. troop-carrying lorries were travelling down to Salcombe and the coast. They were spaced about 50 yards apart, travelled at about forty to 45 miles an hour, and were preceded by a couple of dispatch riders or a jeep. There were so many of them that the column could take up to half an hour to pass.

One morning I had been to Ernest Steers to collect some tines for the hay turner and ran into a convoy at the top of Coombe Royal Hill. The military police in the jeep, headlights on, waved me into a lay-by and the column thundered by. After about a quarter of an hour I was becoming impatient, as there was work to be done at home so I swung my Morris Eight around and joined the column. Because of my intrusion the noise of the claxon horns was deafening as we sped down the hill towards Kingsbridge. I kept close to the vehicle in front so that I could swing off into Plymouth Road at the top of the town, which I did on two wheels.

One afternoon in early May our farm at Woolston was invaded by columns of troop carriers, half-track vehicles, bren-gun carriers and an assortment of other vehicles. Gateways were widened, tents were quickly erected and telephone lines looped through the trees from one field to another. We knew the invasion of Europe was imminent.

Betty and I were married in February 1947 when the countryside was covered in six inches of glistening snow. The blizzard conditions continued for several weeks delaying our honeymoon at the Cumberland Hotel in London.

We were able to rent 90 acres and decided to increase Betty's 400 accredited breeding hens to 2,500 on controlled range, as this was the most profitable branch of farming. Two large incubators hatched thousands of chicks each week for our many customers through South Devon, and this continued into the 1960s when we were able to acquire the two adjoining farms and create a dairy unit for 200 Friesian cows. With the extra commitments of a larger farm the poultry business was gradually discontinued.

It was about this time that Ernest Marples, Minister of Transport, was constructing new motorways and articulated lorries could bring 30 tons of protein/mineral concentrate each month directly to our farm and so we could avoid double handling in and out of store. The local Co-operative would not give a concession for this cost saving so seven farmers joined me in setting up a company, Avon Farmers Ltd., to buy most of our farm requisites.

The business was administered from offices at Lilwell from 1960 to 1963 and during that time the company increased significantly in membership. Scoble's premises in Wallingford Road, Kingsbridge were purchased in 1965 for a base. Branches were soon established in Tavistock and Liskeard and a building section, employing about 25 men, began to build and repair farm buildings. A livestock marketing section was introduced in 1962 with a base at Rake Farm and this was the forerunner of Aune Valley Meat.

A similar company, Mole Avon Trading, was formed at Crediton in 1966 in co-operation with Mole Valley Farmers to service the mid Devon farmers who were situated between our two companies. MAT expanded to cover the Okehampton to Axminster areas. Avon Farmers Ltd. has, in recent years, merged with West Devon and North Cornwall Farmers under the name of Countrywest Trading. During this period I was fortunate to be awarded a Nuffield Scholarship to study dairy farming and poultry breeding in Great Britain and Ireland. It was a

Below: Stacking wine bottles in the cellar after a good harvest in 1990. Each section held 6,500 bottles of wine. They were stacked 32 bottles high and eight bottles deep.

wonderful opportunity to study the most advanced farming practices at that time. I would not have been able to leave our business for three months intensive study without Betty's management and administration nor without Len Wood's care of the pig breeding and bacon unit. Fred Diamond was in charge of the cow unit at that time. He came to us in 1950, and was with us until he retired in 1984. Now he comes occasionally to do some gardening for us.

I was a magistrate on the Kingsbridge Bench for 22 years from 1972 to 1994, which I found to be interesting work.

I was a member of the Country Landowner's Association for a number of years at Devon County level and served on their Agricultural Land Use Committee in London for ten years from 1974. It was a very interesting time as food production in the UK and in Europe was still increasing through animal and cereal genetic improvements, and by modern farming techniques. The Common Agricultural Policy was being evolved within the European Economic Community at that time and I was privileged to be appointed as one of the four delegates to the Confederation of European Agriculture during the nine years from 1976 to 1984. We met annually for a week in one of the European capitals, 500 delegates from all the European Countries discussed agriculture, social and economic problems in four Commissions from education, training, insurance, pure agriculture, and the work of the agricultural Co-operatives in Europe.

In 1972 we planted our first vines at Lilwell as an experiment. The main vineyard was planted in 1977 and extended to ten acres by 1980 as another farming enterprise. The project was very labour intensive and time consuming so our son John took over the general farming enterprise, leaving us to concentrate on the vineyard. After a while Andrew, our eldest son, decided to join us and took care of the vineyard pruning, training and cultivations with the help of Bert Beer and the part-time work of Fred Diamond. It was a challenge to grow crops of grapes in our variable climate but we were encouraged by winning some national awards for our wines. Visitors came on our guided tours, interested in the systems of vine training and in the techniques of wine making which Betty had evolved. Tours ended with a taste of the finished produce in the cellar. The vineyard and wine making provided a stimulating chapter towards the end of our working life.

I have been a feoffee of the local charities for many years. The Arundell Charity was founded in 1591 by Sir Matthew Arundell for 'the good and behoof of the parishioners of Loddiswell' and in 1728 Richard Philips gave farms to provide monies for the least wealthy of the parish. In 1988 the Peek family, formerly of Hazelwood, gave the Blackdown Rings to the Arundell Charity and, we developed it to provided public access to the Iron Age motte and bailey. More recently a small team of us have renovated the Lod's Well, from which the village takes its name.

Loddiswell has always had a thriving community spirit and I have had the pleasure of being closely involved with parish activities, primary school and the church. Since retiring I have had time to study our local history, and have researched the development and structure of our parish over the centuries.

It is said that some people are lucky. I believe luck is the art of evaluating and grasping opportunities as they occur and it is against that criterion I feel that, during my life I have been extremely lucky!